Kuwait

Frontispiece: **Kuwait Towers**

Consultant: Conerly Casey, Associate Professor, Department of Sociology and Anthropology, Rochester Institute of Technology, Rochester, New York
Please note: All statistics are as up-to-date as possible at the time of publication.

Book production by The Design Lab

Library of Congress Cataloging-in-Publication Data
Sonneborn, Liz.
 Kuwait / by Liz Sonneborn.
 pages cm. — (Enchantment of the world, second series)
 Includes bibliographical references and index.
 ISBN 978-0-531-22015-3 (lib. bdg.)
 1. Kuwait—Juvenile literature. I. Title.
 DS247.K8S68 2014
 953.67—dc23   2013026062

6160

Man in Kuwait City

Contents

Left to right: **Boat-builder, man in prayer, camel race, musicians, girls at Kuwait Towers**

CHAPTER 1

Diving for Pearls

ON AUGUST 23, 2012, A CROWD OF PEOPLE GATHERED at an exclusive seaside sports club in the small Middle Eastern country of Kuwait. They were there for one of the country's favorite annual events—the Pearl Diving Festival. That year, about 160 young men had been selected to participate.

With the sun high in the sky and the temperature rising, the young men were dressed in black shorts and crisp white robes called *dishdashas*. Their proud parents stood by as they lined up to shake the hands of government officials and other dignitaries in attendance. Each wished the men the best of luck on the exciting adventure that lay ahead for them. As a band played the Kuwaiti national anthem, the young men said good-bye to their friends and relatives and boarded nine dhows—traditional wooden boats that Kuwaiti sailors used for centuries.

This annual Pearl Diving Festival has been held in Kuwait since 1986. The first annual festival was sponsored by Jaber

Opposite: **Families watch young Kuwaiti men leave to search for pearls.**

KUWAIT

- ● Cities of over 50,000 people
- ○ Other cities
- ✪ National capital

0   30 miles

0   30 kilometers

IRAQ

IRAN

Abdali

Warbah

Rawdatayn

Bubiyan

Sabah al-Ahmad
Nature Reserve

Qasr as-
Sabiyah

Kuwait Bay

Az Zawr

Failaka

Al-Abraq

Kuwait
City

Hawalli

Ad-Dawhah

As-Salimiyah

Al-Jahra

Al-Farwaniyah

Salwa

Persian
Gulf

Qalib al-Shuyukh

Janub
Khaytan

Sabah as-Salim

As-Sulaybiyah

Al-Ahmadi

Al-Fahahil

Mina al-Ahmadi

As-Subayhiyah

Mina Abd Allah

Az-Zawr

Al-Wafrah

Al-Khiran

SAUDI ARABIA

Kuwait

al-Ahmad al-Jaber al-Sabah, the emir, or ruler, of Kuwait
at that time. Since then, the tradition has continued under
the patronage of each new emir, including Sabah al-Ahmad
al-Jaber al-Sabah, who has held this position since 2006. In
2012, Minister of Justice Jamal Shehab represented the emir
at the send-off ceremony. During a speech to the crowd, he
spoke of the festival's importance to the people of Kuwait:
"Celebrating this day expresses our respect to the past and our
traditions."

A Dangerous Profession

The young men sent on the nine-day pearl diving expedition were indeed following a long Kuwaiti tradition. Men have been diving into Kuwait Bay to scoop up oysters, hoping to find pearls inside the shells, at least since the mid-1700s, when Kuwait City, the capital of what is now Kuwait, was founded. The bay's warm, salty waters were particularly hospitable to oysters. The oysters in Kuwait Bay produced a large number of pearls, and the pearls were often bigger and more perfectly round than those harvested in other waters of the world.

A diver shows off the pearls he gathered during the festival.

Kuwait City began as a small settlement in a harsh area. It had almost no fertile soil or freshwater, and for most of the year the climate was incredibly hot and dry. In a region with few other resources, its pearling industry became central to Kuwait's economy and way of life. Merchants there shipped Kuwait's beautifully shaped pearls to far-off lands, where they were made into jewelry and ornaments for the wealthy.

Pearl diving was a dangerous and difficult profession. Divers jumped into the water with beeswax in their ears and clips on their noses to keep water out. They carried baskets to collect

Pearl divers collect oysters from the bottom of the sea. They put the oysters into baskets to bring them back to the ships.

the oysters as they propelled themselves to the seabed, which was often as much as 60 feet (18 meters) below the water's surface. To collect as many oysters as possible, the divers tried to stay underwater for as long as they could. Almost as soon as they came back up to the surface with their catch, they headed back down again. These hardy men sometimes made as many as forty dives in a single day. Many were injured or even killed performing this extremely hard physical work.

Returning Heroes

The job is far less dangerous for the young men who sign up for modern pearl diving festivals in Kuwait. They dive in shallower waters, usually no more than 15 feet (5 m) deep. Their dhows are escorted by ships staffed with paramedics, who are ready to provide medical care in case any of the divers are hurt or suffer exhaustion. Their voyages are also comparatively short, lasting just a few days instead of the many months pearl divers spent at sea long ago.

Even so, the young men have to train long and hard before they can participate in the festival. They are not pearl divers by trade, because there is no longer much of a pearl industry in Kuwait. They, therefore, must go through several months

Dhows are traditional wooden sailing ships used in many parts of Asia. Few trees grow in Kuwait, so dhows there are made from teakwood imported from India.

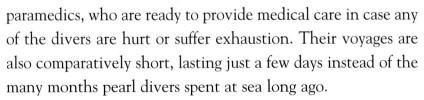

Diving for Pearls **13**

In Kuwait City, dhows are still built using traditional tools and traditional materials.

of instruction by older sailors who show them how to dive and sail a dhow. The instructors also teach the young men old songs that were traditionally sung by pearl divers to comfort themselves during their long months at sea.

Among these treasured songs are ones celebrating the return home. In the past, just returning to dry land was the pearl diver's greatest reward. Today, during the Pearl Diving Festival, the homecoming is an extravagant celebration aired live on national television. The young divers are hailed as heroes as they reveal how many pearls they collected during their trip. In 2012, the harvest of five hundred pearls was particularly impressive. As always, the divers did not keep the pearls for themselves, but instead presented them as a gift to the emir.

A Wealthy Nation

The emir of Kuwait is now incredibly rich, but his wealth comes from oil, not pearls. Oil was discovered in Kuwait in the 1930s. Almost immediately, the discovery transformed Kuwait from one of the poorest countries in the world into one of the richest. The emir and his family are not the only ones to profit from Kuwait's oil reserves. Kuwaiti citizens now have access to well-paying jobs and generous benefits from the government, all funded by oil revenue.

Kuwaitis today live much more comfortable lives than their ancestors did. Only a few generations ago, many Kuwaitis lived in houses built with stone and mud plaster and traveled by camel. Their descendants now live in modern homes, work in skyscrapers, and drive through the glittering capital in luxury cars. In fact, once revenue from oil sales began pouring into the country, nearly everything about Kuwait was transformed—from the makeup of its population to how the people of Kuwait lived to how Kuwait was seen by the other countries of the world.

Pipes carry oil from deep wells in northern Kuwait. About 7 percent of the world's oil lies underneath Kuwait.

Although Kuwaitis enjoy the material comforts of oil wealth, many also feel profoundly uncomfortable with the rapid changes they have seen in their society. Some Kuwaitis, for instance, believe that government benefits have made their people lazy and spoiled. Older Kuwaitis particularly complain that young people do not respect hard work, and value only things that money can buy.

These anxieties explain in part the Kuwaitis' love for the Pearl Diving Festival. As the grandmother of one of the divers in 2012 explained to the *Kuwait Times*: "I think it's great, as it shows the new generation how we lived in the past before the

Kuwaitis enter a raffle for a Mercedes at a shopping mall in Kuwait City.

oil era. I heard from my father about the pearl diving, which was difficult at that time and lasted for many months. Today, everything is easy and the young people should know how their fathers lived."

By honoring Kuwaiti traditions of old, the Pearl Diving Festival provides a brief moment of relief to Kuwaitis overwhelmed by a rapidly changing world. But it does not solve a central question all Kuwaitis face: Can their society retain its ties to the traditions of the past while at the same time embracing all the comforts of the modern world?

Young Kuwaiti women walk along the marina in Kuwait City, which has quickly changed from a fishing village to a city of skyscrapers.

CHAPTER 2

A Desert Land

KUWAIT IS LOCATED IN THE REGION KNOWN AS the Middle East, where Asia and Africa meet. It lies in western Asia, on the northeastern edge of the Arabian Peninsula. Kuwait is a tiny country, extending across only 6,880 square miles (17,819 square kilometers). It is a little smaller than the U.S. state of New Jersey.

Kuwait's Neighbors

Kuwait shares borders with two much bigger nations. To the north and west is Iraq. To the south and west is Saudi Arabia. To the east is Kuwait Bay, part of a larger body of water called the Persian Gulf (also known as the Arabian Gulf). The Kuwaiti coastline stretches approximately 310 miles (500 kilometers).

Kuwait's border with Saudi Arabia was set in 1922, and Kuwait's boundary with Iraq was established soon thereafter. However, Iraq long disputed this border. During late 1990

Kuwait's Geographic Features

Highest Elevation: Unnamed site, 1,004 feet (306 m) above sea level

Lowest Elevation: Persian Gulf, at sea level

Longest Border: With Iraq, 149 miles (240 km)

Shortest Border: With Saudi Arabia, 138 miles (222 km)

Largest Island: Bubiyan, 333 square miles (862 sq km)

Hottest Months: July and August, average daily high temperature of 116°F (47°C)

Coolest Month: January, average low temperature of 47°F (8°C)

Wettest Month: January, average 1 inch (2.5 cm) of rainfall

Driest Months: June, July, August, and September, average 0 inches (0 cm) of rainfall

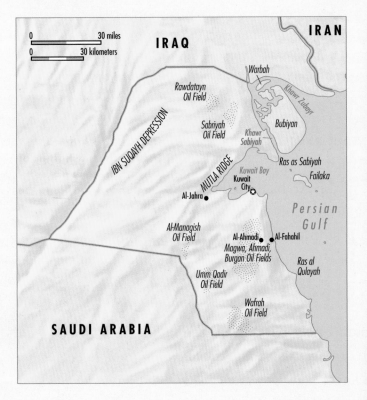

The Neutral Zone

In 1922, an agreement between Kuwait and Saudi Arabia established the Neutral Zone (also called the Partitioned Zone). Measuring about 2,000 square miles (5,180 sq km), this area straddles Kuwait's southern border with Saudi Arabia. Today, these two countries share equally all the money made from the zone's oil reserves.

and early 1991, Iraqi troops briefly took over Kuwait, but a multinational force led by the United States drove them out of the small nation. In 1992, the United Nations, an international peacekeeping organization, created the border that now stands between Kuwait and Iraq.

Al-Wafrah, along the southern border with Saudi Arabia, is one of the few farming areas in Kuwait.

In addition to its mainland territory, Kuwait lays claim to nine islands. The largest is Bubiyan. In the spring, its coastal marshes are home to a beautiful array of wildflowers, making it a popular spot for camping. Bubiyan is also the site of a massive development project. Kuwait's government plans to transform the island into a major shipping center.

Kuwait's second-largest island, Failaka, is of enormous historical importance to the country. The earliest settlements in what is now Kuwait were made on Failaka. They date back as many as four thousand years.

The ancient ruins on Failaka Island are easily visible from above.

Cities of Kuwait

Most of the population of Kuwait lives in Kuwait City and the surrounding suburbs. Very few people live inland, but there are a few other sizable cities located elsewhere along the Kuwaiti coast.

South of Kuwait City is al-Fahahil (below), home to about 74,200 people. This traditional town now functions as a suburb of the capital. Al-Fahahil has a large oil refinery, but it also features a wide variety of shops, malls, and restaurants.

Built in the 1940s and 1950s to house workers in Kuwait's oil industry, al-Ahmadi now has about 41,600 residents. Named after Emir Jaber al-Ahmad al-Jaber al-Sabah, it is the headquarters of the Kuwait Oil Company. Al-Ahmadi is also known for its public gardens and for its large soccer stadium.

Thanks to its freshwater wells, the oasis city of al-Jahra (above) was Kuwait's traditional center of agriculture. Located about 30 miles (48 km) west of Kuwait City, it has a population of about 28,400 and is the capital of the large al-Jahra governorate (a governmental division similar to a state). Al-Jahra is the nation's greenest city, with parks and farms interspersed among its high-rises and villas. It is also home to the Red Palace, one of Kuwait's most important historical landmarks. There, Kuwaiti soldiers battled an invading force from Saudi Arabia in 1920.

Once a River

Today, Kuwait has no permanent lakes or rivers. But images from space satellites suggest that about ten thousand years ago a great river delta covered much of the country. In 1993, Egyptian American scientist Farouk El-Baz presented the theory that an ancient 500-mile-long (805 km) river, with its source in the mountains of western Saudi Arabia, once flowed eastward across the Arabian Peninsula. Called the Kuwait River by El-Baz, it was possibly as much as 3 miles (5 km) wide and covered an even larger area at its mouth, located in present-day Kuwait. El-Baz theorized that volcanic gravel found in much of Kuwait was likely carried there by the river's waters, from mountains hundreds of miles away.

Hot and Dry

Nearly all of Kuwait is desert land. The terrain is largely flat, although low hills are found in some areas. The country's most distinctive geological feature is Mutla Ridge. This row of hills lies just north of Kuwait City, Kuwait's capital and largest city. The top of Mutla Ridge offers an excellent view of Kuwait Bay.

The border of Kuwait is shown on this satellite image. From this view, it is easy to see that Kuwait has no rivers.

As expected in a desert, Kuwait is also very dry. It has no permanent rivers or lakes. However, various places in the country feature *wadis*, low-lying areas that fill with water during the winter rainy season. Traditionally, desert-dwelling nomads called Bedouin used wadis as watering pools for their herds of camels. There are also some marshy areas along the coast.

The lack of sources of freshwater has long posed a problem for Kuwait. In earlier centuries, almost all the country's drinking water had to be imported from other nations aboard large ships, or by camel caravan from what is now Iraq. In recent years, though, Kuwait has invested in desalination plants, which remove the salt from seawater, making it fit to drink. Kuwait today has some of the largest and most technically sophisticated desalination facilities in the world.

For their drinking water, Kuwaitis depend on desalination plants, which remove salt from seawater. The first desalination plant was built in Kuwait in 1951.

With few water sources, it is hardly surprising that Kuwait has very little farmland. But even if it had enough water to irrigate large fields, most of its soil is too salty to grow crops. In fact, less than 1 percent of Kuwait's land can be farmed. As a result, the country has to import nearly all the food needed by its people.

Kuwait sometimes experiences heavy downpours in the winter. Because the parched desert land cannot absorb the water, flooding occurs.

A Harsh Climate

Kuwait is also a forbidding land because of its harsh climate. Its longest season is summer, which can last for six months. From April to September, Kuwait becomes one of the hottest areas in the world, with temperatures rising as high as 130 degrees Fahrenheit (54 degrees Celsius). Because of this intense heat, most buildings in Kuwait are now air-conditioned.

Its brief, warm winter is much more comfortable. For instance, high temperatures in January tend to hover between 50°F (10°C) and 70°F (21°C). During some winter nights, the air can turn quite cold, occasionally dropping to the freezing point (32°F or 0°C).

Winter is also the rainy season. In an average year, Kuwait has an annual rainfall of just about 4 inches (10 centimeters), with most of it falling between

October and March. At times, though, a very heavy rain might bring 2 inches (5 cm) in one day. These cloudbursts can cause flooding and damage roads and homes.

Strong winds from the northwest known as *shamals* sometimes blow over Kuwait. Shamal winds are most common in the summer, especially in June and July, although they sometimes occur during winter. When a shamal strikes, it can whirl sand and dust into the air. During a particularly severe sandstorm, people may not be able to see more than a few feet in front of them.

Heavy sandstorms make it difficult to see more than a few feet in any direction.

Environmental Challenges

Massive sandstorms are just one of the environmental problems facing Kuwait today. The waters along its coast and the air around Kuwait City are fairly polluted. The government is now working toward improving these conditions, but some environmental activists claim it is not doing enough.

Iraqi soldiers set about eight hundred oil wells on fire as they left Kuwait in 1991.

Some of Kuwait's environmental problems are the result of a lack of regulation of its oil industry. But many date back to the end of the Persian Gulf War (1990–1991), during which the Iraqi army occupied Kuwait. In February 1991, an international military coalition forced the Iraqis out of the country. But, on orders from the Iraqi president Saddam Hussein, the soldiers blew up many of Kuwait's oil fields as they retreated. More than one billion barrels of oil were set aflame. The sky was full of dark smoke for months. The poisonous smoke killed trees, birds, and other animals. Many people also contracted serious lung ailments, including cancer, from breathing in the smoke.

The oil that did not burn seeped into the ground, contaminating soil and underground water supplies. Spilled oil also destroyed many beaches. Inland, oil combined with sand to create a hard crust on much of Kuwait's desert lands. In these areas, even the hardy desert vegetation native to the region could no longer survive. In addition, during the war, Iraqi tanks and trucks stirred up and loosened the top layer of the desert's sand. As a result, sand is easily whipped up, and sandstorms are far more common and intense than they were in the past.

An estimated one-third of Kuwait's land was damaged during the war and its aftermath. Iraq's invasion of Kuwait left many scars on the nation and its people. But among the longest lasting was the environmental catastrophe that began during the conflict's final days.

A small bird cannot move because it is covered in oil. The damage to Kuwaiti oil wells at the end of the Gulf War caused oil leaks that killed thousands of birds and other wildlife.

CHAPTER 3

The Natural World

KUWAIT IS NATURALLY A FORBIDDING ENVIRONMENT for both plants and animals. The interior deserts are extremely hot and dry, with so little water that few species can survive there. Kuwait's soil is also sandy and full of minerals, including sodium, making it largely unsuitable for farming. In addition to the damage caused by oil fires and oil spills following the Gulf War, human activities such as overhunting and overuse of grazing lands have made Kuwait less and less hospitable to wild plants and animals.

Vegetation and Agriculture

Despite the environmental challenges, some particularly hardy plant species are still found in Kuwait. Various grasses and small shrubs grow in the desert, especially during the cool winter rains. In spring, several varieties of wildflowers bloom, adding color to the landscape. In marshy areas along the coast grow halophytes, tall grasses that thrive even in Kuwait's salty water.

Opposite: **Camels and sheep graze on the sparse grasses near al-Jahra.**

Desert Beauty

The bright yellow Arfaj is the national flower of Kuwait. A member of the daisy family, it grows on a dense desert shrub. Native to Saudi Arabia and the United Arab Emirates as well as Kuwait, the Arfaj plant can survive with very little water. The flowers bloom in spring, most commonly in April and May. Traditionally, the Arfaj was used to make medicines, feed livestock, and light fires. Because of changes to the plant's environment caused by human activity, there are now far fewer Arfaj blooms brightening up the desert than there were in years past.

Traditionally, the oasis at al-Jahra was Kuwait's agricultural center. Although al-Jahra is now a city, it still has some small farms. Farmers there grow cucumbers, tomatoes, onions, cabbage, and other vegetables. The southern town of al-Wafrah, located along Kuwait's border with Saudi Arabia, is also home to a small farming community. In addition to growing vegetables, al-Wafrah farmers cultivate papaya plants and date palms.

Green Island

Residents of Kuwait City looking for a little greenery need only to stroll over a pedestrian bridge to Green Island. Opened in 1988, the artificial island is full of attractions from a game park to restaurants to outdoor concerts. But for many Kuwaitis, its biggest draw is its well-maintained vegetation. Whether strolling through its gardens or picnicking under a shady tree, many visitors to Green Island enjoy experiencing nature in this very unnatural setting.

Reptiles and Mammals

Many of the animals found in the Kuwaiti desert are snakes, lizards, and other types of reptiles. Among the approximately forty species of reptiles native to the nation are the dab lizard, the sand boa, the horned viper, and the Arabian rear-fanged snake. Scorpions and insects such as the dung beetle are often seen scurrying over the desert sands.

Many larger animals also live in Kuwait, but their numbers have dwindled in recent years because of overhunting. The gazelle and the oryx, for instance, have become all but extinct in the country. Smaller wild mammals that survive in Kuwait include the hedgehog, a small hopping rodent called a jerboa, and a type of cat called a caracal. One of the most unusual animals found in Kuwait is the fennec fox. Among the tiniest

The dab lizard is known for its thick, spiny tail. These lizards grow to be about 1 foot (30 cm) long.

Desert Beast

The national animal of Kuwait is the Arabian camel. It is one of the largest animals found in the country. Camels are perfectly suited to Kuwait's desert lands. Able to draw water from the fat stored in their single hump, they can survive weeks without water, even in stifling summer heat. Their footpads allow them to easily tread across the desert, while their heavy eyebrows and long eyelashes keep blowing sand from getting in their eyes. The Bedouin people who first settled Kuwait traveled by camel.

dog relatives in the world, the fennec fox's body measures only about 1 foot (30 cm) long. It is known for its tall ears and fluffy cream-colored fur.

The fennec fox is well adapted to life in the desert. Its huge ears help heat escape from its body.

Kuwaitis also keep herds of domesticated animals. Farmers often raise goats and sheep for their milk and meat. As their ancestors did centuries before, some desert residents continue to care for camel herds.

Flamingos take flight along the Kuwaiti shore. The feathers of young flamingos are primarily white. They turn pink from pigments in the food the birds eat.

Birds and Sea Life

Perhaps Kuwait's most spectacular wildlife can be seen in the air or in the ocean. Relatively few types of birds live in Kuwait year-round, but around three hundred different species visit Kuwait during their yearly migrations. Birds commonly seen in Kuwait include storks, eagles, hawks, and flamingos.

In Kuwait's coastal waters lives an abundance of marine life. Among the many fish found in the Persian Gulf are cod, shad, pomfret—which is particularly popular in Kuwaiti

A father and son enjoy the aquarium at Scientific Center in Kuwait City.

cuisine—and silver grunts. Other common aquatic creatures near the Kuwaiti coast include lobsters, crabs, sea turtles, and jellyfish. Visitors to the aquarium at Kuwait City's Scientific Center can view these marine animals and many more. The largest aquarium in the Middle East, it is renowned for its floor-to-ceiling tanks filled with stingrays and sharks. Kuwaitis also can see animals from around the world at the Kuwait Zoo. The zoo is home to dozens of species, including elephants, zebras, bears, and lions.

Another favorite spot for animal and nature lovers is the Sabah al-Ahmad Nature Reserve, located just north of Kuwait City. The area's ecosystem was almost destroyed during the Gulf War, when Iraqi soldiers established a military base there.

For more than twenty years, Kuwaiti scientists and conservationists have worked to restore the land that now makes up the reserve. They built ponds and planted trees to attract wildlife native to the desert region. Dotted with purple and yellow flowers in the spring, the reserve is now home to foxes, migratory birds, hedgehogs, and snakes, some species of which are nearly extinct. The restoration of this portion of Kuwait has returned the landscape to its natural state, from before it was ravaged by war and human development.

The Kuwait Dive Team

Founded in 1986, the Kuwait Dive Team is working to preserve and protect the country's marine life. Staffed by volunteers, it takes part in the CoralWatch program.

Coral reefs are made up of the skeletons of tiny creatures called coral polyps. The reefs are vibrant ecosystems, holding a wide diversity of plant and animal life. Coral reefs in the Persian Gulf provide food and shelter for many species of fish and marine life. But in recent years, the health of the coral has been threatened by warming water temperatures and human activities.

The Kuwait Dive Team goes into the waters off the shore to retrieve sunken boats and abandoned fishing nets that threaten the reefs. It also sets up buoys on the water above the coral, so that boats do not accidentally damage the reefs with their anchors. The members of the Kuwait Dive Team consider education an important part of their mission. The group hopes to inspire young Kuwaitis to join the fight to protect the country's fragile marine environment.

CHAPTER 4

Old and New

I T IS NOT KNOWN FOR CERTAIN WHEN HUMAN BEINGS first came to live in what is now Kuwait. Most likely the earliest people there did not settle on the mainland, but instead on Failaka Island, the second largest of the nine islands that now belong to Kuwait. People were living on Failaka by 2000 BCE, but there may have been a settlement on the island even earlier. Archaeologists—scientists who study how ancient people lived—have found pottery, tools, and stone walls left behind by these early inhabitants.

By about 2300 BCE, the Dilmun civilization had emerged on the island of Bahrain in the Persian Gulf. Dilmun merchants established a number of trading outposts, including one on Failaka. The merchants there probably traded with the people of ancient Mesopotamia (now Iraq) and Persia (now Iran). Later, in about the third century BCE, Greek soldiers and sailors built a small trading post on Failaka, which they called Ikaros. Archaeologists have unearthed the remains of ancient Greek temples on the island.

Opposite: **This sculpture of a head of a bull was found in a temple from the Dilmun culture.**

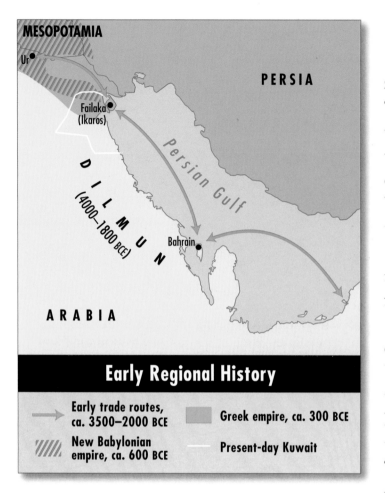

MESOPOTAMIA

Ur

PERSIA

Failaka
(Ikaros)

Persian Gulf

D I L M U N
(4000–1800 BCE)

Bahrain

ARABIA

Early Regional History

→ Early trade routes,
ca. 3500–2000 BCE

▨ New Babylonian
empire, ca. 600 BCE

▨ Greek empire, ca. 300 BCE

— Present-day Kuwait

Settling Kuwait City

The region that is now Kuwait was once known as Khadima. It was a stopping point for camel caravans making the long trek between Europe and points farther east in Asia. For centuries, it was part of this vital trade route. Over time, however, it fell into disuse.

In the early 1600s, members of the Bani Khalid tribe established a small fishing village on the coast of what is now the Kuwaiti mainland, where the caravans once stopped. The Bani Khalid were desert dwellers called Bedouin. The Bedouin were nomads—people without a fixed home, who traveled from place to place. They survived largely by raising livestock, including goats and sheep. But their lives revolved around their herds of camels. Because the harsh deserts of the Arabian Peninsula had very little vegetation and water, the Bedouin were always on the move, heading to the next place that would have food and freshwater for their animals.

Probably in 1672, Barrak bin Ghuraif, leader of the Bani Khalid, built a fort at what is now Kuwait City. The area became known as *kuwait*, meaning "little fort."

Excavating Failaka Island

Kuwait's Failaka Island is one of the most intriguing archaeological sites in the Middle East. It has been visited by teams of archaeologists from Poland, France, Italy, and Denmark—all looking for buried artifacts that might shed light on the island's four thousand year history. Among their most interesting discoveries were the ruins of several churches dating from the eighth and ninth centuries.

Late in the seventeenth century, the center of the Arabian Peninsula experienced an extreme drought. The Bedouin were hardy people, used to scraping by in the forbidding desert. But, without rainwater, living there became nearly impossible. Members of the Bani Utub tribe decided they had to move

Bedouin relax in the shade of a tent in the Kuwaiti desert.

for their survival. Beginning in about 1710, they headed to the coast and eventually took over the settlement at Kuwait. At first, they maintained a seminomadic way of life. In the summer, they lived at the settlement, but in the winter, they headed inland to pasturelands to feed their herds.

Soon, however, several families at the settlement began to take advantage of the coastal location. They learned how to fish, dive for pearls, and, most importantly, build and sail ships called dhows. This knowledge allowed them to become merchants in international trade. A few families began to amass great wealth. Among them was the al-Sabah family. Its members took over the collection of taxes from desert cara-

A fruit seller in the 1910s in Kuwait City. Kuwait has long been an important trading site.

Mubarak the Great

Born in 1840, Mubarak al-Sabah, also known as Mubarak the Great, is today considered the father of modern Kuwait. His father Abdullah al-Sabah (Abdullah II) served as the ruler of Kuwait during the late nineteenth century. After his death in 1892, Mubarak's older brother Muhammad became Kuwait's new ruler, although he worked closely with his brother Jarrah. Muhammad placed Mubarak in charge of trying to keep peace with the Bedouin tribes living inland.

Perhaps Mubarak feared Muhammad and Jarrah were plotting against him. Or possibly, he believed that a distant relative, Yusuf ibn Abdullah al-Ibrahim, was about to try to wrest control of Kuwait from Muhammad, who was proving to be a weak leader. Whatever Mubarak's motivation, contemporary accounts hold that, with the help of his sons Jaber and Salim, Mubarak assassinated his brothers Muhammad and Jarrah, and named himself the ruler of Kuwait.

With the backing of the powerful Ottoman Empire, Yusuf tried to challenge Mubarak's claim to the throne. To protect Kuwait and his position, Mubarak negotiated an agreement with Great Britain, which promised to provide military protection for the country.

In addition to dealing with the Ottoman threat, Mubarak also helped develop Kuwait. He established schools, oversaw the opening of the country's first hospital, and created a postal service. Ever since the death of Mubarak the Great in 1915, the ruler of Kuwait has always been a direct descendant of one of his two sons.

vans and trade ships visiting Kuwait, a job that placed them in a powerful position. In 1756, a council of men from the most important families in Kuwait met to choose a leader. They selected Sabah bin Jaber, the man then in charge of the al-Sabah family. Ever since, Kuwait has been ruled by members of the House of al-Sabah.

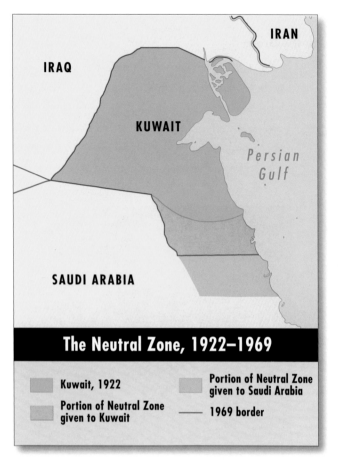

IRAN

IRAQ

KUWAIT

Persian
Gulf

SAUDI ARABIA

The Neutral Zone, 1922–1969

Kuwait, 1922

Portion of Neutral Zone
given to Kuwait

Portion of Neutral Zone
given to Saudi Arabia

—— 1969 border

Powerful Neighbors

By the nineteenth century, powerful neighboring nations began eyeing tiny Kuwait and its wealth. The Ottoman Empire, which controlled much of Asia and part of Europe, seemed especially eager to annex Kuwait.

The ruler of Kuwait, Mubarak al-Sabah (also called Mubarak the Great) skillfully handled the threat posed by the Ottoman Empire. In 1899, he brokered a secret deal with Great Britain in which he promised not to give territory to or negotiate with another foreign power. In exchange, the British vowed to protect Kuwait from its enemies. At the time, Great Britain was a powerful empire that ruled over many lands, including India in Asia. Kuwait would remain a British protectorate for more than sixty years.

Struggling for Control

In the early twentieth century, Europe and the United States came to believe that there were vast oil reserves in the Middle East. They began struggling to ensure that they got a share of this oil. After World War I, France and Britain dismantled the Ottoman Empire and divided Arab territories into spheres of influence.

In the early 1920s, an army of Bedouin warriors led by Faisal al-Dawish of Najd, present-day Saudi Arabia, invaded Kuwait. Al-Dawish claimed that Kuwait rightfully belonged to his country. With help from British troops, Kuwait drove out the Najd forces. But the victory came at a price. In the peace treaty the British negotiated in 1922, Kuwait was compelled to surrender about two-thirds of its territory. The following year, the British also set the border between Kuwait and Iraq.

These colonial boundaries frequently proved controversial, especially after oil was discovered. In 1938, Iraq tried to reclaim Kuwait as part of Iraq, and the Kuwaiti Parliament voted to rejoin Iraq, but the emir dissolved parliament. The imposed national boundaries also made it difficult for Iraq to gain access to the Persian Gulf to export its oil.

From Pearls to Oil

Much of the 1930s was a bleak time for Kuwait. Trade was disrupted by the Great Depression, a worldwide economic

The Red Palace

Today, very few structures of historical importance in Kuwait are still standing. A rare exception is the Red Palace. Located in al-Jahra, about 30 miles (48 km) west of Kuwait City, the Red Palace is a large rectangular fort. It was probably constructed in the late nineteenth century by Mubarak the Great, the ruler of Kuwait at that time. Built from mud bricks, the fort has thirty-three rooms and six courtyards. The structure is most famous for its role in the Battle of al-Jahra in 1920. During the conflict, Najd forces from what is now Saudi Arabia briefly took control of the Red Palace before being expelled by Kuwait's ruler Salim al-Mubarak al-Sabah and his army. The Red Palace got its name from the rose hue of its bricks, but folklore maintains it was stained that color by the blood of the Kuwaitis who fought and died there. The Red Palace is now a historical museum.

After oil was discovered in Kuwait, roads had to be built through the empty desert to reach drilling sites.

downturn. At the time, Kuwait's most important export was natural pearls, which were harvested from oysters in coastal waters. During the Depression, few people had the money to buy luxury goods, so the demand for pearls dropped sharply. But the pearling industry was dealt an even bigger blow by Japan, which then began producing cultivated pearls at a cheaper price.

The country's fortunes improved after the Kuwait Oil Company (KOC) was founded in 1934. Controlled by American and British investors, it began drilling for oil in Kuwait. By 1938, so much oil was discovered that Kuwait became a very rich country virtually overnight.

When it became clear that the Kuwaiti royal family did not intend to share the oil wealth, several rich merchants became concerned. They feared the Kuwaiti people, already suffering because of the economic depression, would rise up in rebellion. These merchants organized the Majlis Movement and established their own lawmaking assembly as a challenge to the House of al-Sabah. Ahmad al-Jaber al-Sabah dissolved the assembly, but, bowing to pressure, created a new council to advise the ruling family.

Oil drilling in Kuwait was interrupted by World War II (1939–1945). But after the war, the KOC quickly built new wells and pipelines. By 1947, it was pumping 16 million barrels of oil a year. By 1953, it was producing more oil than any other nation in the Persian Gulf region.

Ahmad al-Jaber al-Sabah ruled Kuwait from 1921 to 1950. During his reign, the nation's borders were set and oil was discovered.

In 1950, Abdullah al-Salim al-Sabah (Abdullah III) became the new ruler of Kuwait. As oil revenues poured in, he proved himself a forward-thinking ruler, using a sizable portion of Kuwait's riches to benefit its people. Before the discovery of oil, the only schools in the nation were a handful of private schools for boys. Under Abdullah III, the nation developed a modern and comprehensive educational system. It offered free education from kindergarten to secondary school for both Kuwaiti boys and girls. Similarly, very few Kuwaitis had access to medical care before 1950. But using money gained through oil exports, the government led by Abdullah III began providing free health care to every Kuwaiti citizen.

Kuwait also spent lavishly to improve its infrastructure. During this period, the country built its first network of paved roads. It also constructed power plants to provide electricity and desalination facilities to produce fresh drinking water.

An Independent Nation

During this time, Kuwait's population was booming, in large part because of an influx of foreign laborers. As the need for skilled professionals grew, Kuwait encouraged the immigration of educated and trained workers from other nations. Many workers in the oil industry, for instance, were from Great Britain. The teachers in Kuwait's new school system were largely from Palestine, while medical professionals from Egypt made up much of the staff in Kuwaiti hospitals.

Low-skilled foreign workers were also brought in to perform jobs that Kuwaitis no longer wanted to do, such as cleaning

and construction. The government offered jobs, often very high-paying ones, to any Kuwaiti citizen who wanted them. Because of their access to good government jobs, traditional ways of earning a living, such as animal herding and fishing, were virtually abandoned.

Oil money also ushered in another great change for Kuwait—the end of its dependence on Great Britain. Under an agreement between Kuwait and Britain, Kuwait became a fully independent nation on June 19, 1961. The next year, the country ratified its constitution—a written document that sets out the rules by which a country is governed. According to the constitution, Kuwait's ruler, called an emir, had to be a member of the al-Sabah

After the discovery of oil, Kuwait City grew quickly. Here, pedestrians cross a street jammed with cars in 1956.

Kuwaiti soldiers run through the desert during a training exercise in 1961.

family. But the constitution also provided for an elected lawmaking body called the Majlis al-Umma, or National Assembly. Only men who could prove they had had family living in Kuwait in 1920 could vote for assembly members.

The Iraq-Iran War

Kuwait had won its independence, but it had lost the protection provided by its allegiance to the British. Mindful that Kuwait was a small, rich nation surrounded by large, powerful countries, Abdullah III had spent years building up its army, navy, and air force. Despite his efforts, Kuwait's independence was immediately challenged by Iraq, which laid claim to Kuwait and its oil wealth. When Iraq threatened to invade, Kuwait asked Britain for military assistance. A British force gathered in Kuwait. It was later bolstered by soldiers sent by the Arab League, an organization of Arab nations that Kuwait had joined in 1961. Iraq backed down and formally recognized Kuwait's independence.

Even with its tense history with Iraq, Kuwait sided with this enemy when war broke out between Iraq and Iran in 1980. Kuwait saw Iran as the greater threat. A year earlier, a revolt in Iran led by a religious leader called Ayatollah Khomeini had overthrown the Iran government. Kuwaiti elites were alarmed by Khomeini's vow to spread revolution to other Arab countries. As a result, during the Iran-Iraq War (1980–1988), Kuwait loaned Iraq the equivalent of about US$13 billion. The Kuwaiti government also allowed Iraq to transport military supplies across its land. Because of

Jaber III served as minister of finance and economy and as prime minister before coming emir.

Kuwait's pro-Iraq stance, a terrorist group that supported Iran attempted to assassinate Kuwait's emir Jaber al-Ahmad al-Jaber al-Sabah (Jaber III) in 1985. Iran also attacked Kuwaiti ships and oil tankers in the Persian Gulf.

During the war, Kuwait tried to strengthen its ties to its friendly neighbors. In 1981, it joined Saudi Arabia, Bahrain, Qatar, Oman, and the United Arab Emirates to form the Gulf Cooperation Council. The member nations promised to work together to deal with common security and economic concerns. Kuwait also sought assistance from the United States, whose navy helped protect Kuwaiti vessels.

Despite Kuwait's support of Iraq, the relationship between the two countries fell apart after the war. For many years, Kuwait and Iraq had battled over the Rumaylah oil field, which spread across the border between the two countries. Saddam Hussein, the president of Iraq, accused Kuwait of stealing oil from the field that rightfully belonged to Iraq. He also accused Kuwait of blocking Iraqi access to the Persian Gulf and revived earlier claims that all of Kuwait was actually part of Iraq's territory. Using these justifications, he ordered the Iraqi army to invade Kuwait on August 2, 1990.

The Gulf War

The Iraqi ground force that invaded Kuwait included about 120,000 soldiers and two thousand tanks. In the early morning hours, they crossed the border and headed toward Kuwait City. With the small Kuwaiti army powerless to stop them, the Iraqis barreled through the country, and by noon they had taken over the capital. The Iraqis had planned to capture the emir, but he escaped to Saudi Arabia.

The United Nations (UN) immediately condemned Iraq's invasion. The organization imposed economic sanctions on the country, which meant that no country represented at the UN would buy oil from Iraq. The UN hoped that Saddam Hussein, unable to sell the Kuwaiti oil he had seized, would be compelled to retreat. Several nations also sent ships to the coast to form a blockade so no goods could be shipped in or out of Kuwait.

Soon after the invasion, the United States began planning a military strike against Iraq to liberate Kuwait. Wanting to make the attack an international effort, American diplomats and politicians worked to persuade other nations to support and aid the mission. Eventually, they created a coalition of thirty-four nations, including Great Britain, France, Saudi Arabia, Egypt, Bahrain, and the United Arab Emirates. They assembled a force of more than six hundred thousand troops.

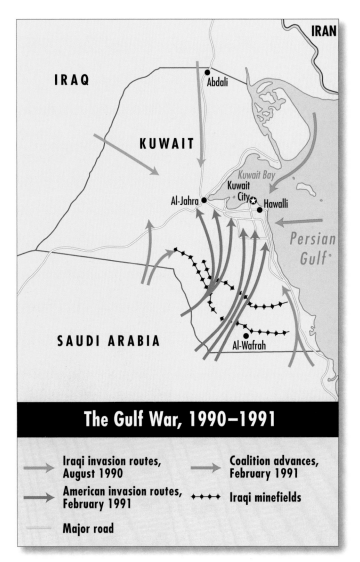

The Gulf War, 1990–1991

→ Iraqi invasion routes, August 1990

→ American invasion routes, February 1991

— Major road

→ Coalition advances, February 1991

✦✦✦✦ Iraqi minefields

A Brutal Occupation

The Kuwaiti people suffered greatly during their nation's occupation by Iraq. Iraqi soldiers rounded up everyone they thought might mount a resistance movement. The people they arrested were subject to brutal interrogations and were sometimes tortured. Many were then sent to prisons in Iraq. Others were executed in front of their families. Iraqi soldiers also routinely stole possessions and destroyed houses owned by Kuwaitis. During the six-month occupation, about half the total population of Kuwait fled the country.

The military campaign began with a series of air attacks on the morning of January 17, 1991. Coalition warplanes bombed hundreds of targets a day, including airfields, ammunition bases, railroads, bridges, and areas where Iraqi troops were stationed. Military planners hoped that the massive air campaign would make Saddam Hussein end the occupation, but he refused to withdraw the Iraqi troops.

U.S. forces roll through the desert on the way to the Kuwaiti border during the Gulf War.

On February 24, the coalition escalated the conflict with a ground invasion. When the coalition army entered Kuwait from Saudi Arabia, many Iraqi soldiers quickly surrendered. In just three days, coalition troops reached Kuwait City. They gave the honor of liberating the capital to the Martyrs Brigade, one of several units of Kuwaiti fighters who had joined the campaign.

After the War

For the next few days, everyone in Kuwait City gathered in the streets to celebrate the Iraqi retreat. But the Iraqi soldiers did not go quietly. As they headed back to Iraq, they set fire to hundreds of oil wells.

Kuwaitis also had to deal with destruction caused by both the occupation and the war. The Iraqi soldiers had destroyed, damaged, or looted many buildings and institutions. For instance, they set Kuwait University ablaze, stripped hospitals

A man votes in parliamentary elections in 1992. Of the people eligible to vote, about 83 percent went to the polls that year. That was a much higher number than usual.

the occupation living in luxury in Saudi Arabia. Understandably, many of the Kuwaitis who suffered through the occupation resented the fact that Jaber III had run away during his country's bleakest hour. Although Jaber III was restored to his leadership position, many Kuwaitis wanted to limit his authority and to give more power to elected officials. Because they opposed the old style of government, they became known as the opposition.

Under pressure, Jaber III called for the election of a new National Assembly in October 1992. About two-thirds of those elected were from the opposition. Only one-third were pro-government representatives who supported the emir. Not only did the opposition and pro-government factions have very different ideas of how Kuwait should be governed, but different groups among the opposition also disagreed with one another. For instance, some opposition leaders were liberals who wanted radical reforms, such as allowing women to vote in elections. Others were conservatives who wanted Kuwait to be a very traditional society based closely on the teachings of Islam, the national religion. Ever since this election, the tensions between the emir and the National Assembly and between the factions within the opposition have been heated.

Into the Future

As Kuwait headed into the twenty-first century, it had mostly rebounded from the catastrophe of the Iraqi invasion and the Gulf War. Its economy was growing, and its infrastructure had

Skyscrapers dominate the Kuwait City skyline.

been largely rebuilt and modernized. In addition, one of its most pressing concerns—a possible second invasion orchestrated by Iraq's president Saddam Hussein—was resolved unexpectedly in 2003. Along with a small coalition of nations, the United States, claiming that Iraq had illegal weapons, invaded Iraq and removed Hussein from power. Unlike most Middle Eastern nations, Kuwait was a strong supporter of this military action. Leading up to the invasion, the government of Kuwait allowed the coalition forces to establish bases in Kuwait, from which they staged their attack.

Although Hussein is gone, Iraq continues to present a problem for Kuwait. The invasion of Iraq sparked a civil war

American soldiers pulled down a statue of Iraqi leader Saddam Hussein in Baghdad, the capital of Iraq, after forcing him from power in 2003.

there, leaving the nation politically unstable. At the same time, Kuwait has ongoing concerns about Iran, which has been accused of trying to develop nuclear weapons. In 2011, tensions increased between the two countries when an Iranian spy ring was found to be operating in Kuwait.

The political volatility of the entire region became clear in early 2011, when many nations near Kuwait saw a wave of protests and demonstrations. This popular movement, called the Arab Spring, sought major reforms in how these countries were governed. In Kuwait, some demonstrators took to the street, charging that the government was corrupt. Desperate to tamp down the revolutionary fever, the government sent out payments worth US$3,600 and vouchers for eighteen months of free food to each Kuwaiti citizen. Calls for reform, however, remain as loud as ever. In the future, Kuwait will have to face two extremely difficult challenges—how to deal with its neighboring nations and how to reform its government in a way that satisfies the majority of its people.

Kuwaitis took to the streets in 2013 to protest the jailing of opposition leader Musallam al-Barrak for insulting the Kuwaiti emir Sabah al-Ahmad al-Jaber al-Sabah.

CHAPTER 5

The State of Kuwait

SINCE KUWAIT BECAME AN INDEPENDENT NATION in 1961 it has been governed as a constitutional emirate. The constitution of Kuwait lays out the powers and responsibilities of its three branches of government—executive, legislative, and judicial. The head of the executive branch holds the title of emir. The emir of Kuwait has always been drawn from the powerful al-Sabahs, who have been the country's ruling family since about 1756.

The Executive Branch

The emir is Kuwait's head of state. He has the power to appoint the prime minister, who is the head of the government and therefore responsible for overseeing its day-to-day workings. In the past, the emir himself was the prime minister, but beginning in 2003 the jobs have been given to different members of the al-Sabah family. Today, the prime minister is usually next in line to become the new emir when the current emir dies or resigns from his position.

A Look at the Capital

According to Kuwait's official census, the capital of Kuwait City has only about 32,400 residents. But this figure counts only the people living in the city center. When the surrounding suburbs are taken into account, Kuwait City's population is about 2,400,000. In fact, the majority of people living in Kuwait reside in the Kuwait City metropolitan area.

Located on the southern shore of Kuwait Bay, Kuwait City was founded in the mid-1700s and soon became an important trading center. But nearly all evidence of the city's history is now gone. The old walls surrounding Kuwait City were torn down during the period of rapid growth after Kuwait began exporting oil in 1946. Today, only the iron gate from the city walls stands as a monument to the past.

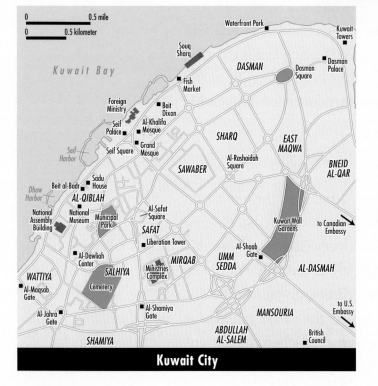

Kuwait City

Kuwait City is not just the capital. It is also Kuwait's leading financial and cultural center. It is a gleaming modern city, filled with sky-scrapers and high-rise apartment buildings. Throughout Kuwait City, there are lively restaurants, crowded coffee shops, world-class museums, well-maintained parks, and luxury shops. It is also the home of Kuwait University, the National Assembly building, and the Seif Palace, where Kuwait's ruler, the emir, lives.

The city's most famous landmark is the Kuwait Towers. The highest of these three steel towers rises to 614 feet (187 m). On this tower are two huge spheres decorated with glittering blue and green stones. The lower sphere houses several restaurants, while the higher one contains a rotating observation deck that provides spectacular views of the city and the Persian Gulf.

For decades, the emir has been a direct descendant of Mubarak al-Sabah, who ruled Kuwait from 1896 to 1915. Traditionally, the post of emir alternated between two branches of the al-Sabah family. One branch traced its descent back to Mubarak's son Jaber; the other, back to Mubarak's son Salim. More recently, however, the al-Sabah family has not always followed this rule in choosing the emir.

The emir and the prime minister are assisted in their duties by the Council of Ministers. The prime minister recommends candidates for the council, but they have to be approved by the emir. Each minister is in charge of a different area of government. For instance, Kuwait has ministers who oversee defense, foreign affairs, health, communications, commerce and industry, and oil. Many of the ministers are from the al-Sabah family or from other wealthy and influential families who were traditionally part of the merchant class. In 2005, Massouma al-Mubarak

The offices of the emir and prime minister are located in Seif Palace. The clock tower atop the palace is a Kuwait City landmark.

was named the minister of planning and administration. She was the first female minister in the history of Kuwait.

The emir has a great deal of power under the constitution. In fact, he can suspend parts of the constitution or even the entire document at any time for any reason. If he is displeased with the decisions being made by the National Assembly, he can simply send its members home. In recent decades, the emir has frequently dissolved the National Assembly. According to the constitution, the emir must hold a new election within ninety days of invoking this power, but in practice, emirs have often ignored this rule.

Massouma al-Mubarak has served as the minister of planning and administration and the minister of health. In 2009, she became one of the first four women to win seats in the National Assembly.

The National Assembly

The Majlis al-Umma, or National Assembly, meets in one of the most distinctive buildings in all of Kuwait. It was designed by Danish architect Jorn Utzon. The National Assembly building's sweeping roof honors Kuwait's history by evoking the tents of the Bedouin, the nomadic people who were the early settlers of Kuwait City.

The National Assembly consists of approximately sixty-five members. Fifty are elected by popular vote. The rest of the assembly is made up of council ministers. Up to fifteen min-

National Government of Kuwait

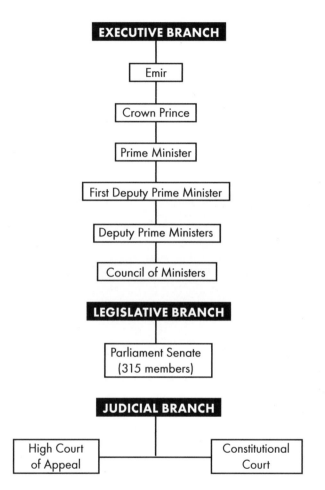

EXECUTIVE BRANCH

Emir

Crown Prince

Prime Minister

First Deputy Prime Minister

Deputy Prime Ministers

Council of Ministers

LEGISLATIVE BRANCH

Parliament Senate
(315 members)

JUDICIAL BRANCH

High Court
of Appeal

Constitutional
Court

isters can serve. All elected members can vote on legislation, but there are some restrictions on the voting rights of ministers in the assembly. Established by the Kuwait constitution, the National Assembly is the oldest elected legislature in any Arab country. If the emir does not dissolve the assembly early, it meets for four years before there is a new election.

In addition to voting on new laws, the National Assembly serves as a check on the executive branch. The assembly can summon ministers and other officials and question them about their actions and policies. These interviews, which are often lively and heated, ensure that ministers cannot completely ignore the priorities of Kuwait's elected officials. In extreme cases, the National Assembly can even vote to remove council ministers or the prime minister from office.

Kuwait's National Assembly meets in a modern building in Kuwait City.

Kuwait's National Anthem

Since 1978, the song "Al-Nasheed al-Watani" ("National Anthem") has often been performed during national holidays in Kuwait. The anthem's lyrics, which pay tribute to both Kuwait's founders and its emir, were written by poet Ahmad Meshari al-Adwani. Ibrahim Nasir al-Soula wrote the music.

English translation

Kuwait, my country, be safe and glorious!

Always enjoy good fortune!

You were the home of my ancestors, who wrote your history,

With everlasting equality, through all eternity.

Those Arabs were holy.

Kuwait, my country, be safe and glorious!

Always enjoy good fortune!

Blessed be my country, a harmonious homeland,

Protected by true guardians of the soil,

Creating your history, Kuwait, my country.

We support you, my country,

Led by faith and loyalty,

Within your emir equally, surrounding us all

With warm love and truth.

Kuwait, my country, be safe and glorious!

Always enjoy good fortune!

Elections in Kuwait

In Kuwait, almost any Kuwaiti citizen twenty-one and older can vote in elections for the National Assembly. The exceptions are prisoners and people serving in the military or on a police force, as they are forbidden to vote by law. Technically, foreigners who have become naturalized citizens and have lived in Kuwait for more than thirty years also have the right

A Kuwaiti woman votes in elections in 2012. Since gaining the right to vote in 2006, women have usually made up more than half the voters in Kuwaiti elections.

to vote. However, because few foreign workers stay in the country for more than thirty years, the number of naturalized citizen voters is extremely small. Also, because almost no foreign workers can vote, more than half the people living in Kuwait have no say at all in its government.

Until just a few years ago, only male Kuwaiti citizens could vote. After many years of campaigning, women were finally given the vote in 2006. That year, women could only vote in municipal (city) elections, but the next year, they were permitted to cast ballots for the National Assembly. The turnout of women voters was unexpectedly small, however, and no female candidate was victorious. In 2009, however, four women became the first female members of the National Assembly.

In Kuwait, the law forbids the formation of political parties. However, there are some political groups that more or less function the way parties do in democratic countries such as the United States and Canada. Among the most powerful groups are those

A noted economist and women's rights activist, Rola Dashti became one of the first women elected to Kuwait's National Assembly in May 2009. Born in 1964, Dashti attended Johns Hopkins University in the United States, where she studied economics. Returning to her native country, she worked at the Kuwait Institute for Scientific Research and the National Bank of Kuwait. Elected the Chairman of the Kuwait Economic Society, Dashti became the first woman to hold this prestigious position.

Active in Kuwait's women's rights movement, Dashti was a leader in the campaign to allow women to vote in Kuwaiti elections. After women were granted voting rights in 2006, she was the first Kuwaiti woman to register to vote. In the historic 2009 election, Dashti and three other women became the first female members of the National Assembly, Kuwait's legislature. As Dashti explained in 2010, "Kuwaitis were extremely joyful about having women in [the National Assembly]. . . . But with that joy come[s] high expectations; people see women as saviors, as the ones who will bring real change." Dashti was later named to the Council of Ministers, and served as both the minister of Planning and Development and the minister of National Assembly Affairs.

representing traditional Muslims. In opposition to them are secular reformers. They want to modernize the government, but do not feel that reforms have to conform to religious tradition. Other groups are pro-government. They strongly support the emir, the royal family, and other elites with positions in the executive branch.

محكمة التمييز
محكمة الاستئناف
المحكمة الكلية
النيابة العامة

A lawyer talks on his cell phone outside Kuwait's Constitutional Court. This court interprets the country's constitution.

The Judicial System

Several levels of courts make up Kuwait's judicial branch. Criminal and civil cases are tried in the same court system, while those involving family law are considered in special courts. The highest court in the land is the High Court of Appeal. The emir, however, has the final say in punishments handed down by judges. The constitution gives him the right to pardon a prisoner or reduce his or her sentence.

The emir is also responsible for appointing judges. If an appointee is a Kuwaiti citizen, that person holds the position for life. But most of the judges in Kuwait are foreigners. They are appointed for a shorter term, usually one to three years.

In cases involving personal status such as marriage, divorce, and inheritance, Kuwaiti courts rely on Sharia, or traditional

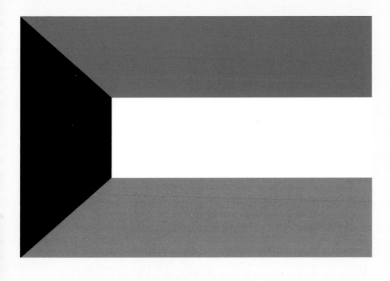

The Flag of Kuwait

The Kuwaiti flag features three horizontal bands—a green one on top, a white one in the middle, and a red one on the bottom. On the left side of the flag appears a black trapezoid, a four-sided figure with only two parallel sides. The flag of Kuwait is similar to the flag of Arab Revolt, which was adopted by many Arab nations in the early twentieth century. That flag, however, uses black for its top band, green for the middle, white for the bottom, and has a red triangle to the left. On Kuwait's flag, green stands for fertile fields, white for purity, red for blood on Kuwaitis' swords, and black for the defeat of the nation's enemies.

Islamic law. Sharia law tends to favor men over women. For instance, in Kuwait's family courts, a judge gives a woman's testimony only half the legal weight of a man's. Family courts are also divided into three types—one for Sunni Muslims, one for Shi'i Muslims, and one for non-Muslims.

Reforming the Government

In recent years, the government of Kuwait has instituted several important reforms to make it more responsive to its citizens. Giving women the vote helped involve many more people in the electoral process. The man named as emir is no longer also named as prime minister, which makes it easier for the National Assembly to hold the prime minister accountable for his decisions.

Other reforms have dealt with newspapers, television, and other media. The government now allows more outlets for news than it did in the past. However, the press is not free to print or broadcast whatever it wants. The government prohibits the media from criticizing the emir or Islam. It also restricts anything that might be deemed immoral or likely to spread discord among different groups of people in Kuwait. Kuwait also blocks Internet sites that government censors feel do not conform to these rules.

Violating these rules can land a journalist in prison. In the past, most reporters have censored themselves, so few were prosecuted. Such prosecutions have been on the rise in recent years, however, as Kuwaitis have grown more vocal in their disagreements with the emir and his inner circle.

In 2011, large crowds took to the streets of Kuwait City to protest the emir's regime. Many were young people who accused the government of being corrupt. They demanded a more fair and open government. Other protesters belonged to Islamist opposition groups that had long been critical of the ruling family, which tends to have a secular approach to government. The Islamists want a strict interpretation of Islam to play a greater role in Kuwaiti law and society. In response to the massive unrest, the prime minister resigned and the emir dissolved the National Assembly.

The election of a new assembly took place in February 2012. Leaders of opposition groups, especially Islamists, took many seats. The emir was unhappy with the results, and the Constitutional Court took the unprecedented step of declaring the election void. Before the next election, the emir changed the voting laws to the benefit of pro-government candidates. Many opposition leaders urged voters to boycott, or sit out, the election.

With a very low turnout of voters who favored the opposition, the December 2012 election put into office many representatives who strongly supported the emir.

The political struggles of 2011 and 2012 illustrate one of the greatest challenges facing Kuwait. The growing tension between the emir and the National Assembly make it nearly impossible for the country to deal with crucial issues. Kuwait is a rich country with plenty of money to solve its most pressing problems. But unless the emir and the elected assembly can work together, in the years to come Kuwait will see little real change, except perhaps in the attitudes of Kuwaitis craving reform. As their frustration grows, the people will likely become even more aggressive in the demands for a new and better form of government.

In 2012, protesters took to the streets with signs urging Kuwaitis to boycott the upcoming election. They argued that changes to the electoral system favored pro-government candidates and were unfair to the opposition.

CHAPTER 6

A Land of Oil

TODAY, KUWAIT IS ONE OF THE RICHEST COUNTRIES in the world. Its capital is full of dazzling modern skyscrapers, and its citizens enjoy a high standard of living, which includes free health care, free college tuition, and easy access to good-paying jobs. These benefits are all funded by oil, which remains at the center of Kuwait's economy.

The Oil Industry

Experts estimate that approximately 7 percent of the world's oil reserves lie beneath Kuwait. Currently, the country produces about 2.5 million barrels of oil a day. The country could continue at that rate of production for at least 150 years before running out of oil.

With such a valuable natural resource, it is hardly surprising that the economy of Kuwait is almost wholly based on the oil industry. It is managed by the Kuwait Petroleum Corporation, the country's national oil company. Since 1975, the company has been owned and operated by the government of Kuwait. Its revenues account for more than half of

What Kuwait Grows, Makes, and Mines

AGRICULTURE (2009)

Fruits	15,642 metric tons
Vegetables	220,966 metric tons
Milk	275,876 metric tons

MANUFACTURING (VALUE ADDED, 2012)

Refined oil products	US$4,969,600,000
Chemical products	US$2,231,500,000
Food and beverage products	US$463,500,000

MINING

Oil (2010)	2,500,000 barrels per day
Natural Gas (2010)	51,000,000 cubic meters per day
Ammonia (2009)	485,000 metric tons

the money the government takes in each year. The rest is earned largely from overseas investments Kuwait made in the past with oil money. The Kuwaiti government earns so much income from oil exports and investments that it does not require its people to pay any taxes.

Although not as lucrative as oil, natural gas has also long played a significant role in Kuwait's economy. In 2006, its importance grew with the discovery of large reserves of gas in the northern portion of the country. Kuwait now produces about 1.8 billion cubic feet (51 million cubic meters) of natural gas a day. Locally, Kuwait uses natural gas to power electric plants and water desalination facilities.

Other Industries

Oil and gas production drive Kuwait's economy, but increasingly the country is investing in other industries. Products made in Kuwait include cement, fertilizer, and petrochemicals (chemicals produced from petroleum or natural gas). Kuwait exports these goods to other countries in Asia and Europe.

Fishing and shrimping were once a thriving sector in Kuwait's economy. Although the country does produce some seafood, because of pollution in the Persian Gulf, these are no longer significant industries.

Fish are laid out at a seafood market in Kuwait City. Popular fish include grouper and pomfret.

Agriculture is now almost nonexistent in Kuwait. In fact, farming is responsible for far less than 1 percent of Kuwait's gross domestic product, or the total worth of goods and services produced in the nation each year. As a result, the country has to import just about all of the food it needs. Kuwait also relies on trading partners for clothing, automobiles, wood, and other construction materials. Most of these goods come from Kuwait's political allies, including the United States, Japan, and Germany.

Traditionally, tourism has not played much of a role in Kuwait's economy. However, the country is trying to attract more vacationers to its beautiful beaches. There are now more

Families relax on the beach in Kuwait. Nearly three hundred thousand foreign visitors arrive in Kuwait every year.

than a dozen luxury hotel resorts in Kuwait. They cater largely to travelers from other Arab countries.

The Kuwaiti Workforce

In recent decades, Kuwait has used its oil income to provide generous social services to its citizens. The government provides Kuwaitis with cheap housing, free health care and education, guaranteed retirement income, and often gifts of money and food. As a result, many Kuwaiti citizens can afford not to work. Only about half of Kuwaitis hold jobs. More than nine out of ten citizens who do work are employed by the government.

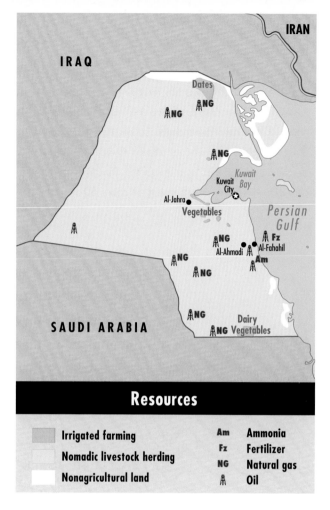

Resources		
Irrigated farming	Am	Ammonia
Nomadic livestock herding	Fz	Fertilizer
Nonagricultural land	NG	Natural gas
	⚒	Oil

In the past, Kuwaiti women were expected to work at home, keeping house and raising their children. But increasingly, they are moving into the workforce. About one-third of Kuwaiti women now work outside the home. By law, however, there are some jobs they cannot perform. Women are forbidden from holding positions in the military and from holding some jobs that are considered too physically dangerous for them.

The majority of workers in Kuwait are not Kuwaiti citizens. A small number are Americans and Europeans hired by Kuwait's oil industry for their technical expertise. Americans

The government of Kuwait has recently tried to develop new industries, because its officials are worried about the country's economic dependence on oil. As part of this effort, Kuwait is encouraging citizens to become entrepreneurs and start their own businesses. The government provides entrepreneurs with grants of about 80 percent of the cost of starting a business. If the business fails, the entrepreneur does not have to pay back the money. The system allows people to start a business with very little personal risk. Still, few Kuwaitis take the government up on its offer. Most Kuwaitis have kept their government jobs because they are secure and pay well.

and Europeans also work in private schools and universities. Many highly educated Arabs, particularly from Palestine, Syria, Egypt, and Lebanon, have moved to Kuwait to work in the educational, legal, health, and building industries. Unskilled foreign laborers work in sales, cleaning, construction, and domestic labor. They perform the menial and service jobs that Kuwaitis are not willing to take. Most of these workers are from South, Southeast, and East Asia. They are primarily from Bangladesh, India, Pakistan, Sri Lanka, Indonesia, Thailand, the Philippines, and more recently, China. In all, about 80 percent of the people in Kuwait's workforce are non-Kuwaitis. Unlike Kuwaiti citizens, they receive only limited financial help from the Kuwaiti government.

In recent decades, the treatment of some foreign workers has become an issue. In particular, women who work as household servants suffer from poor working conditions and often endure physical abuse. While activists are working to improve the lot of foreign workers, the government is trying to reduce their numbers. Concerned that more than half the population of Kuwait is made up of foreigners, the government has repeatedly set up policies designed to keep non-Kuwaitis out of the country. The

citizens of Kuwait, however, continually thwart these efforts. Their demand for foreign laborers who are often willing to perform unpleasant work for very little pay is just too high.

Construction workers stand with supplies at a site in Kuwait. The vast majority of workers in Kuwait come from other countries.

Transportation and Communications

The Iraqi occupation of Kuwait in 1990 and 1991 was a disaster for the country in many ways. One of the most important economic legacies of that era is the country's infrastructure. After the Iraqi soldiers retreated in 1991, Kuwait was left in ruins. But because so much of the nation had to then be rebuilt almost from scratch, its transportation and communication systems are all very modern.

Kuwait has an extensive system of roads that are well used. Nearly all families in Kuwait own cars. The roads of Kuwait, especially in the capital, are often clogged with traffic. Many foreign workers travel around the country in comfortable air-conditioned buses.

CHAPTER 7

Citizens and Foreigners

After oil was discovered in Kuwait more than seventy years ago, the nation's population quickly began to rise. Except for during the Iraqi occupation, it has been booming ever since. According to the Kuwaiti government, there are more than 3.3 million people living in the country.

Kuwait is one of the most urbanized countries in the world. About 98 percent of its people live in cities. The vast majority are residents of Kuwait City and its suburbs.

Young and Old

Kuwait has a fairly young population, in part because a sizable number of older people did not survive the Iraqi occupation and its aftermath. The median age of the Kuwaiti people is twenty-nine, and about 30 percent of the population is younger than fifteen. Because of Kuwait's excellent health care system, life expectancy is high. A baby born in Kuwait today can expect to live to be seventy-seven.

Population of Major Cities (2012 est.)

Kuwait City (metropolitan area)	2,400,000
Al-Fahahil	74,200
Al-Ahmadi	41,600
Al-Jahra	28,400

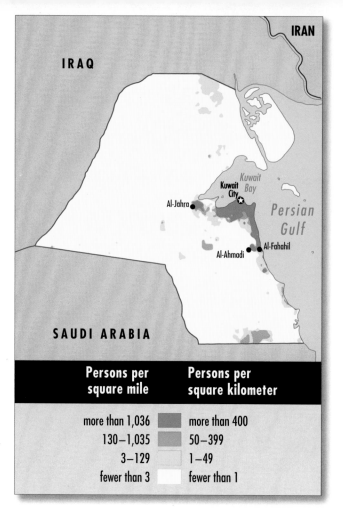

Persons per square mile

Persons per square mile		Persons per square kilometer
more than 1,036		more than 400
130–1,035		50–399
3–129		1–49
fewer than 3		fewer than 1

Ethnic Groups in Kuwait

Kuwaiti	45%
Other Arabs	35%
South Asian	9%
Iranian	4%
Other	7%

Arabs and Others

The majority of people in Kuwait are Arabs. Most Kuwaiti citizens are the descendants of the Arab desert peoples who established settlements in the mid-eighteenth century in what is now Kuwait City. Other Arabs in Kuwait are from nearby Middle Eastern countries, such as Egypt and Syria. Non-Arab foreigners in Kuwait include large numbers of people from Iran and South Asia.

The people of Kuwait have long included many foreigners. Some work as doctors, engineers, and teachers. Others are unskilled laborers, who find jobs as housekeepers, drivers, and construction workers.

In Kuwait's early years as an independent nation, many of its foreign workers were from Palestine. Often, they and their families had called Kuwait home for decades. But the Kuwaitis turned against the Palestinian immigrants after the Iraq occupation of the early 1990s. The government of Palestine supported Iraq's invasion of Kuwait. As a result, many Kuwaitis believed, often without proof, that Palestinian workers within their borders also approved of Iraq's actions. After the liberation of Kuwait, its government forced many Palestinians to leave the country.

"Without Nationality"

About 120,000 residents of Kuwait are *bidoon jinsiya*, Arabic for "without nationality." Often called Bidoon, they are not citizens of Kuwait or anywhere else. They are people without a country. Unlike official Kuwaiti citizens, Bidoon do not receive generous benefits from the government. They cannot work legally, attend free Kuwaiti government schools, or get passports for travel. They are without rights, and without options.

The families of many Bidoon lived in Kuwait when the nation became independent, but they failed to register for Kuwaiti citizenship. Some could not read and write. Others did not hear about the need to register for citizenship or understand what was at stake. Now, decades later, they are still suffering.

In recent years, protests have grown to try to gain more rights for Bidoon and foreign workers. In 2013, the Kuwaiti Parliament passed a law giving four thousand Bidoon people citizenship. But many more still wait.

Social Rank

Foreign workers now make up well over half of the total population of Kuwait. The situation has created a rigid class structure in the country. At the very top of society are the emir, the royal family, and other elites descended from the wealthy merchants who founded Kuwait. They are incredibly wealthy and live in luxury.

Below them are the rest of Kuwait's citizens. From birth to death, they are entitled to generous government benefits.

Below these Kuwaitis are the educated, well-paid foreigners who work in the oil industry and in professions. They are generally treated with respect by Kuwaitis. Some are even granted Kuwaiti citizenship if they live in the country long enough.

Far below them in social stature are the other foreigners, who usually have low-paying, low-prestige jobs. These people receive few benefits from the Kuwaiti government and few protections under law. Often Kuwaiti employers take advantage of these workers. They might pay workers very little or

A Kuwaiti woman with her Indian servant. Many Kuwaitis do not treat foreign workers as respectfully as they treat other Kuwaitis.

even not pay them at all. Foreigners are sometimes forced to work extremely long hours and are given little food. No matter how poorly they are treated, they cannot look to the legal system for help. Many foreign workers are treated well and have warm feelings toward their adoptive country. But others are fed up with their unequal treatment and have joined protests against the Kuwaiti government.

The Languages of Kuwait

Arabic is the official language of Kuwait. Virtually all Kuwaiti citizens speak Arabic. A sizable number of foreign workers also know the language. Arabic is written using the twenty-eight-character Arabic alphabet. It is written and read from right to left.

English is the second most common language used in Kuwait. Business dealings, especially in the oil industry, are sometimes conducted in English. The language is also taught in many schools. Arabic is the language of instruction in Kuwaiti government schools, but classes are taught in English in private schools and universities. Young people often want to learn English so that they can study in the United States and Great Britain.

Signs at the Kuwait City airport are in both Arabic and English.

CHAPTER 8

Spiritual Life

ISLAM IS THE OFFICIAL RELIGION OF KUWAIT. NEARLY all Kuwaiti citizens are Muslims, or followers of Islam. Many noncitizens living in Kuwait are Muslims as well, although a sizable number of foreigners there observe other faiths.

The Prophet Muhammad

Islam had its beginnings in the seventh century with the teachings of a traveling merchant named Muhammad. Born in Mecca in what is now Saudi Arabia in 570, Muhammad is said to have been visited by the angel Gabriel at about age forty. Muslims believe that the angel communicated to him the word of God, which is "Allah" in Arabic.

Muhammad, who is called the Prophet, began to share the messages he had received with others. His followers took down these messages and compiled them into the Qur'an, the holy book of Islam. As Muhammad's influence spread, authorities in the region feared he was becoming too powerful. Suspecting that his enemies would try to assassinate him, Muhammad fled from Mecca to Medina, also in today's Saudi Arabia, a journey that Muslims call the Hijra.

Islam continued to spread, even after the Prophet's death in 632. Today, it is the second most popular religion in the world, after Christianity. More than 1.2 billion people are Muslims.

Sunni and Shi'i Muslims

After the Prophet died, a dispute arose concerning who should be the caliph, his successor as the leader of all Muslims. Sunni Muslims believed that the caliph should be chosen from a group of elites. Shi'i Muslims held that he should be a direct descendant of Muhammad.

The division between Sunni and Shi'i Muslims has continued into the present day. Approximately 80 percent of the world's Muslims today belong to a Sunni sect. The majority of Muslims in Kuwait, including the members of the royal family, are Sunnis. However, the exact numbers of Sunni and Shi'i Muslims are not known because the Kuwaiti census does not collect this data.

Reciting the Qur'an

Mishari Rashid Alafasy is internationally acclaimed for his recitations of the Qur'an, the holy book of Islam. Born in Kuwait in 1976, Alafasy studied the Qur'an at the Islamic University of Medina in Saudi Arabia. Through his studies, he became a noted qari. Qaris recite portions of the Qur'an, often from memory, following specific rules for proper pronunciation. Alafasy frequently appears on television and has made many recordings. He also serves as the imam of the Grand Mosque in Kuwait City.

Although estimates vary, probably about 70 percent of Kuwaiti Muslims are Sunni, while the remaining 30 percent are Shi'i.

In Kuwait, the government monitors the operation of all Sunni mosques (Islamic houses of worship). It appoints Sunni imams (Muslim religious leaders) and pays for the construction of any new Sunni mosques. Shi'i mosques, however, do not receive government funding. They are financed exclusively by the Shi'i community.

Practicing Islam

For Muslims in Kuwait, their religion helps shape their relationships, their values, and their day-to-day lives. Like Muslims everywhere, Kuwaiti Muslims do not eat pork or drink alcohol. Kuwaiti Muslims also observe the Five Pillars of Islam. The first pillar is *shahadah*, which requires Muslims to accept the statements "There is no God but God; Muhammad is the messenger of God." The second is *salah*. It says that Muslims should suspend their daily activities five times a day to pray. The call to prayer is issued from minarets, high towers that rise above mosques. When praying, Muslims kneel and bow while facing in the direction of Mecca, the holy city of Muhammad's birth.

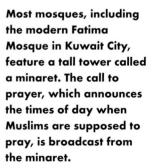

Most mosques, including the modern Fatima Mosque in Kuwait City, feature a tall tower called a minaret. The call to prayer, which announces the times of day when Muslims are supposed to pray, is broadcast from the minaret.

The third pillar of Islam, *zakat*, calls for Muslims to give money to the poor. The fourth, *sawm* requires them to fast, or abstain from food and water, during the holy month of Ramadan.

Hajj, the final pillar, obliges all Muslims to visit Mecca at least one time in their lives if they are able to.

Kuwaiti Muslims must also observe certain religious holidays. The longest is Ramadan, which takes place during the ninth month of the Islamic calendar. During Ramadan, Muslims cannot eat or drink while the sun is out. They eat only a small breakfast before dawn and an evening meal after sunset. In Kuwait, it is illegal for Muslims and non-Muslims alike to eat, drink, or smoke cigarettes in public during daylight hours in the month of Ramadan. Ramadan is meant to help Muslims focus on spiritual reflection. It also encourages self-discipline and concern for those who are less fortunate.

At the end of this long fast, Muslims celebrate the feast of 'Id al-Fitr. During this holiday, they are allowed to eat the foods and treats they denied themselves during Ramadan. They also exchange presents and visit with friends and family. Kuwaiti Muslims also observe 'Id al-Adha, or the feast of sacrifice. During this solemn holiday, people remember the story of the prophet Ibrahim in the Qur'an. Known as Abraham in the Bible, Ibrahim was so devout that he was willing to sacrifice his son when God asked him to do so. This holiday reminds Kuwaitis of the needs of other, less fortunate people. Islamic New Year, the birthday of the Prophet, and the day commemorating Muhammad's ascension to heaven are also national holidays in Kuwait.

Kuwaiti men begin a meal at sunset during Ramadan.

Other Religions

Nearly all non-Muslims in Kuwait are noncitizens. Many are recent immigrants who still practice the dominant religion of their native lands. The most common religions in Kuwait aside from Islam are Hinduism, practiced by about 600,000 residents, Christianity, practiced by 450,000 residents, and Buddhism, practiced by 100,000 residents. Small numbers of people also follow other faiths, such as Sikhism and Bahaism.

The Kuwaiti government formally recognizes several Christian faiths, including the Roman Catholic Church,

The feast of 'Id al-Fitr often includes trips to amusement parks and other fun activities.

the Greek Orthodox Church, and the Anglican Church. The government allows these groups to operate churches in Kuwait, although their activities are closely monitored. However, some Christian religions—including the Church of Jesus Christ of Latter-Day Saints and the Seventh-Day Adventist Church—are not recognized by Kuwait. Christians of these churches are permitted to practice their faiths in private homes, as long as the buildings are not marked with signs or symbols such as the Christian cross.

Members of the royal family attend a special mass at a Greek Orthodox church in Kuwait City following the death of the emir Jaber III in 2006.

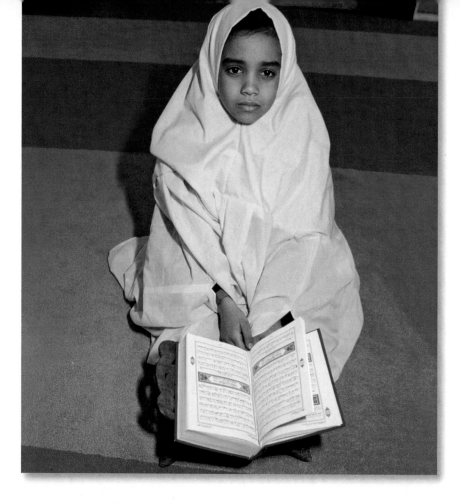

A young girl reads the Qur'an in a class at a mosque. The Qur'an is always recited in Arabic, regardless of the language a person usually speaks.

Hinduism, Buddhism, Sikhism, and Bahaism are similarly not recognized. People of these faiths are forbidden from building permanent places of worship in Kuwait.

Religious Freedom

According to the Kuwait constitution of 1962, Islam is the official religion of the country. But the document also states that Kuwait supports freedom of religion, as long as non-Muslim religious practices do not disrupt public order or offend Muslim values.

Despite this commitment to religious freedom, the government actively works to promote the practice of Sunni Islam. It requires that all public school students receive Islamic religious instruction based on Sunni beliefs. If a private school has at least one Muslim student, it must also provide classes about Islam, although non-Muslim students are not required to attend them.

Many laws enforced in Kuwait limit freedom of expression in order to protect religious values. For instance, it is illegal to defame any religion or to make disrespectful remarks about religious figures such as Muhammad or Jesus. Journalists writing in newspapers and magazines are most commonly prosecuted under these laws, but officials have also targeted people making comments on social media, such as Facebook or Twitter. In one recent case, Shi'i blogger Hamad al-Naqi was convicted of blasphemy and sentenced to ten years in prison for making negative remarks on Twitter about Sunni leaders in Syria and Bahrain.

Conservative members of the National Assembly of Kuwait attempted to make blasphemy a crime punishable by death, but the Council of Ministers blocked the effort. In late 2012, however, the emir issued the National Unity Law. This

Television Controversy

In the fall of 2011, the television series *Banat al-Thanawiya* (High School Girls) sparked a controversy in Kuwait. Based on a series of novels by Kuwaiti author Mohammed al-Nashmi, the series tells the story of five Kuwaiti teenage girls from different backgrounds. The show was scheduled to air in Kuwait during the holy month of Ramadan, until several conservative politicians began speaking out against it. Without having seen the program, one condemned the show as portraying "Kuwaiti schools as dens of vice and corrupt manners, making the girls appear to be lewd and shameless." By the standards of American television, *Banat al-Thanawiya* was fairly tame in its presentation of teenagers. But, as the controversy suggests, Islamists in Kuwait are increasingly attacking popular culture—particularly its depiction of independent women and girls—as a way of drumming up support for their political and religious views.

measure increased the severity of punishments for those convicted of making public remarks offensive to religious groups.

Growing Tensions

Most Kuwaitis are tolerant of people of all religious faiths. But recently, a vocal minority of Islamists has opposed the presence of non-Muslims in Kuwait. Many are affiliated with the political group Adala Bloc. Members of Adala Bloc in the National Assembly attempted to close all Christian churches in Kuwait. When that measure failed, they tried to prohibit the construction of any more churches, even though Christians in Kuwait complain that there are not enough churches to accommodate their needs.

Foreign workers attend a service at a Catholic church in Kuwait City. There are an estimated 140,000 Catholics in the country.

Shi'i Muslims pray at a mosque in Kuwait City.

Tensions are also rising between the Sunni majority and the Shi'i minority. Shi'i Muslims complain that they are often treated like second-class citizens. For instance, in the police force and military, Shi'i are allowed to serve, but they rarely are promoted into high-level positions.

Shi'i Muslims are also upset about the lack of mosques for people of their faith. Of the roughly eight hundred mosques in Kuwait, only about thirty-five are for Shi'i Muslims. The government also does not allow schools in Kuwait to train Shi'i imams, which limits the number and power of Shi'i religious leaders in the country.

Sunni and Shi'i Muslims have lived together peacefully since the earliest settlements in what is now Kuwait. Tensions sometimes arise, however. Conflicts have emerged when political or religious leaders attempt to use religious differences to further their own political agendas.

CHAPTER 9

Kuwaiti Culture

SINCE THE DISCOVERY OF OIL IN KUWAIT, THE country's culture has changed rapidly. In a land full of luxury cars and cell phones, many Kuwaitis fear that their old ways might be lost forever. As a result, the government generously funds efforts to preserve and celebrate Kuwait's cultural traditions. By sponsoring museums, theaters, and other cultural institutions, Kuwait works to ensure that future generations will appreciate the nation's history and artistic heritage.

Opposite: **Drums are an important part of traditional Kuwaiti music.**

Kuwaiti Museums

Several important museums in Kuwait commemorate the hardships the Kuwaitis suffered during the country's occupation by Iraq. The Kuwait House at the National Memorial Museum provides visitors with a sense of how Kuwaitis felt during the invasion. Walking down dark corridors, the visitors are barraged with bright lights simulating gunfire and loud sound effects mimicking helicopters whirring over-

The Tareq Rajab Museum displays antiquities from around the Middle East. The elaborate doors into the museum are from Egypt.

head. Al-Qurain Martyrs' Museum is a memorial to all of the Kuwaiti lives lost during the occupation. It was constructed on the site of the headquarters of a group of young Kuwaitis who fought against the Iraqi occupiers. The museum recounts how Iraqi soldiers bombed and machine-gunned the building for more than ten hours, killing many of the resisters inside.

Before the Iraq occupation, the Kuwait National Museum had one of the finest collections of Islamic art in the world. The Iraqis, however, looted the museum of its treasures and set fire to the building. Since then, some of the stolen works of art have been returned. But only a small portion of the museum building has been renovated and reopened to the public. About two thousand objects are on display, including ancient artifacts found at the early settlements on Failaka Island. Outside the museum is the *Muhallab II*, a full-size replica of a dhow, the type of ship once used by Kuwaiti merchants.

The small Tareq Rajab Museum fared far better during the occupation, owing to some quick thinking by its founder, who was Kuwait's first minister of antiquities. He had the entrance bricked over before soldiers reached the building, protecting the

treasures it stored. The museum has an excellent collection of Islamic pottery, jewelry, metalwork, and musical instruments. It also houses an important library of Arabic manuscripts.

The mission of the Sadu House in Kuwait City is to preserve the arts and crafts of the Bedouin, the desert people who first settled the nation. The cultural center documents Bedouin folktales and dances and features examples of the Bedouin's traditional woven cloth. Sadu House recruits Bedouin women to teach classes in weaving to keep this tradition alive.

Bedouin carpets often include geometric patterns. They sometimes also feature animal figures.

Traditional Songs

Many of the traditional songs of Kuwait are associated with its earliest industries, such as pearling, fishing, and shipbuilding. Songs sung by working sailors were particularly exuberant. When the sailors returned home after a long voyage, they sang songs accompanied by drums and tambourines. Because Kuwaiti sailors

House of Mirrors

One of Kuwait's most unique museums is in the Kuwait City suburb of Qadisiya. Called the House of Mirrors, this museum is the home of Lidia al-Qattan, the Italian widow of Kuwaiti painter Khalifa al-Qattan. Long ago, Lidia al-Qattan accidentally broke a mirror and used the pieces to decorate a cabinet. Her husband was so impressed by her work that he encouraged her to continue. Eventually, she covered all the walls and furniture in the house with mosaics made from more than seventy-five tons of mirrors. Lidia al-Qattan now opens her magical, glittering house to visitors, and it is one of the most popular tourist attractions in Kuwait.

came in contact with other lands, their songs often were influenced by music they heard in other nations in Asia and Africa.

While many old songs and dances have disappeared, some are still performed, especially on national holidays. One example is a dance called al-Fareesa, which features a female dancer dressed as a man, sitting on a horse-shaped box decorated with beads and gold jewelry. During the dance, the rider rocks the "horse" back and forth to avoid an attack by another female dancer brandishing a sword.

During religious celebrations, specially trained men and women sing *mawlids*. The lyrics of these songs tell stories about the life of the Prophet Muhammad. They are most often sung during the festivities held on the Prophet's birthday and the night that celebrates his ascension to heaven. From time to time, the audience responds to the singers with the words "*Hai Allah*," meaning "Allah is everlasting."

Music, Art, and Literature

In addition to their traditional songs, Kuwaitis enjoy many modern styles of music. One favorite is *sawt*, which was popularized by the Kuwaiti performer Shadi al-Khaleej in the 1970s.

Sawt music is played on the oud (a Middle Eastern lute), drums, and violin. Because of the large number of foreigners living in Kuwait, popular music from many different countries can be heard in Kuwait. Kuwaiti singers and musicians now perform in a variety of styles, from pop to rock to hip-hop.

Since 1958, the Kuwaiti government has supported visual artists by sponsoring an art show each spring. Many of the

Musicians play folk music at a performance in Kuwait City.

works are now in the collections of the Modern Art Museum, which opened in 2003. The museum displays the work of noted Kuwaiti artists, such as sculptor Sami Mohammed and painters Jafar Islah and Ayoub Hussein. In 2012, a controversial show by Lebanese artist Tarek Atoui examined the Kuwaiti people's treatment of Palestinian immigrants after the Gulf War, leading many Kuwaitis to reexamine this period in their history.

Kuwait has had a long literary history. Traditionally, Kuwaiti literature focused on poetry, but increasingly writers

A Reality Television Superstar

Young Kuwaiti singer-songwriter Bashar al-Shatti won international fame in 2004 when he appeared in *Star Academy*, a singing competition televised across the Middle East. Born in 1982, al-Shatti studied piano and guitar before appearing on the program at age twenty-one. He immediately became a celebrity throughout Kuwait.

Declaring reality television a corrupting influence, many traditional religious leaders in Kuwait denounced *Star Academy*. They urged the National Assembly to ban the show and demanded that Kuwaitis refuse to watch it. Despite their protests, the people of Kuwait remained fascinated by al-Shatti, who became, in their minds, a symbol of national pride. Although viewers used their cell phones to cast more than one million votes for al-Shatti on the final day of the competition, he came in second, losing to Egypt's Mohammed Attiyeh. Al-Shatti has remained popular in Kuwait as both a recording artist and a television actor.

The 99

have been drawn to short stories and novels. Laila al-Othman has written numerous short story collections, while Ismail Fahd Ismail has written more than twenty novels. In 2013, thirty-two-year-old novelist Saud Alsanousi became the first Kuwaiti to win the International Prize for Arabic Fiction, which is awarded annually to the best novel published in Arabic. Alsanousi's winning book, *The Bamboo Stalk*, tells the story of a half-Kuwaiti, half-Filipino man trying to find his place in modern Kuwaiti society.

The government of Kuwait must review and approve every book before it can be published. In the past, government censors allowed the publication of books on nearly every subject, no matter how controversial. But in recent years, censors have been banning more books, usually on the grounds that they are offensive to socially conservative Muslims.

Theater, Film, and Television

Live theater thrives in Kuwait, in large part because of financial support from the government. In addition to professional productions in Kuwait City, local theater groups often come together during holidays to perform shows. The Kuwait

In the past, young boys typically served as the jockeys in camel races in Kuwait. Now, small robots ride the camels.

Little Theater in al-Ahmadi is the oldest community theater in the Middle East. Founded in 1953 by foreign workers in the oil industry, it produces a variety of plays and musicals each year, performed by amateur actors in English.

The first film made in Kuwait was *Bas ya Bahar* (*The Cruel Sea*), directed by Kuwaiti filmmaker Khalid al-Siddiq. It tells the story of pearl divers in Kuwait before the discovery of oil and is now considered a classic of Arabic cinema. Today, however, there is no real film industry in Kuwait. There are numerous movie theaters in Kuwait City, but they show foreign films. The movies are often heavily edited by the government to remove romantic or violent scenes.

The government of Kuwait owns and operates Radio Kuwait, which broadcasts programs in both Arabic and English. The state-owned Kuwait Television offers four channels that feature news, entertainment, and sports programming. In addition, Kuwaitis can watch or listen to a variety of radio and television shows broadcast by satellite.

Sports and Recreation

Before oil was discovered in their nation, Kuwaitis enjoyed a wide variety of sports. With most of the population living along the coast, swimming and diving in the clear gulf water kept people cool in the summer heat. Camel racing and horse racing were popular with both riders and audiences. In recent years, many Kuwaitis have started attending camel races, where they find betting on the race is just as exciting as watching the camels run. Another traditional sport is falconry—hunting with falcons and other birds of prey—but generally, only wealthy men have had the time and money to indulge in this pastime.

A Kuwaiti man holds his falcon. In a falconry competition, trainers have their birds engage in hunting games.

Kuwait's falconry tradition lives on in the name of its national hockey team. The Kuwaiti Falcons are the only team in the Middle East with membership in the International Ice Hockey Federation. They play home games in an Olympic-size rink in the heart of Kuwait City.

British workers in the oil industry introduced the sport of cricket to Kuwait in the mid-twentieth century. The game is played in a large open area, with players using flat bats to hit a ball. In 2005, the Kuwait Cricket Association became an associate member of the International Cricket Council.

An Olympic Champion

One of the greatest target shooters in the world, Fehaid al-Deehani is the only Kuwaiti athlete to win a medal at the Olympics. Born in 1966, al-Deehani began shooting rifles and shotguns for sport when he was just six years old. With his older brother, he improved his target shooting skills at a shooting club in the city of al-Ahmadi. After graduating from a military college in 1988, al-Deehani devoted all his time to this sport.

During his long career, he has won more than ninety medals and awards in international shooting competitions. But the most prestigious are his two Olympic bronze (third place) medals. Al-Deehani won his first bronze medal during the 2000 Olympic Games in Sydney, Australia, and his second at the 2012 games in London, England. At the London Olympics, al-Deehani also had the honor of carrying the Kuwaiti flag during the opening ceremonies—an event that he found nearly as exciting as winning his medal. He told the *Kuwaiti*

Times, "This was a very emotional moment for me. When we entered the stadium and Kuwait's name was announced, I kissed that flag." After winning his second Olympic medal, al-Deehani considered giving up shooting, but urged on by the emir of Kuwait, he decided to continue training for the 2016 Olympic games.

Kuwait's Abdulaziz Mohammad moves past a Qatari player during an international basketball game.

Basketball is another Western sport embraced by the Kuwaitis. The national team has regularly played in the International Basketball Federation Asia Championship. Its best showing in the competition came in 1983, when the Kuwaiti team won fourth place.

Although there are many basketball fans in Kuwait, the country's most popular sport is soccer, which is called football in much of the world. The Kuwait Football Association has national teams for both men and women that are invited to play in international competitions. In 2011, Kuwait's men's team won the West Asian Football Federation Championship for the first time. The following year, Kuwait hosted the competition at the al-Sadaqua Walsalam Stadium in Kuwait City, where the teams from Kuwait and nine other Asian countries lost the trophy to Syria.

CHAPTER 10

The Kuwaiti Way of Life

THE FIRST KUWAITIS WERE NOMADIC PEOPLE OF THE desert. Today, nearly all Kuwaitis are city dwellers, with most living in Kuwait City and nearby suburbs. Kuwaitis generally live in small houses, although the wealthiest are likely to own large, luxurious mansions. Low-paid non-Kuwaiti workers usually have modest apartments in high-rise buildings.

The camel—once a common mode of transportation—has long been replaced with the automobile. For many, owning a luxury car is an important symbol of their status in society. In such a car-loving culture, it is hardly surprising that traffic jams are common, especially in Kuwait City.

Opposite: **A Kuwaiti father holds his son. Kuwaiti families have an average of 2.5 children.**

Family Life

Kuwaiti families are extremely close-knit. Often, members of several generations live under the same roof. But in recent years, roles in the family have changed dramatically. Traditionally, women spent most of their time caring for their husbands and children. Increasingly, they are now taking jobs outside the home and living more independent lives.

Kuwaiti college students celebrate the end of a year of studying in the United States. More than two thousand Kuwaitis study at American colleges each year.

In the past, children spent their days playing in and around their house with handmade toys. Favorite toys included models of Kuwaiti houses and small ships they could race in the waters along the shore. Today, they are most likely to spend their time at home watching television, playing video games, or surfing the Web. Now, the government requires that all Kuwaiti children between the ages of six and fourteen attend public school, so they are away from their families for much of their childhood. College and university students often travel to other countries to study and sometimes do not see their parents and other relatives for years.

In addition to having strong ties to their relatives, Kuwaitis also maintain close relationships with their friends and neighbors. Kuwaiti families take great pride in their hospitality, and frequently invite friends to their homes for a meal or a visit.

Al-Mohaibis

Today, Kuwaitis often spend their leisure time watching television, going to a theater or museum, or taking strolls through a park. But in the past, they enjoyed playing a variety of traditional games. One favorite game was Al-Mohaibis. The game was played by two teams, alternating turns. Each turn, a member of one team hid a ring in his or her hand. The other team got a point if it correctly guessed who had the ring. The team with the most points at the end of the game won. After the game, all the players sat down together to enjoy an array of treats.

The Diwaniyah

A tradition long embraced by the Kuwaitis is the *diwaniyah*, which means "meeting" in Arabic. During a diwaniyah, a group of men gather in a tent outside the host's home. A wealthy Kuwaiti man might have a special room in his house just for holding *diwaniyat* (the plural of diwaniyah). There, the guests lounge on carpets and pillows while they chat, play games, eat snacks, and drink coffee flavored with the spice cardamom.

Men play cards in a diwaniyah. These meetings are the center of men's social, political, and business life in Kuwait.

Choosing Spouses

In the past, Kuwaiti parents would select suitable spouses for their sons and daughters, often with the help of a professional matchmaker. They wanted to make sure their children married into a family with the same social status or a higher social status than their own. Today, many young people want to choose their own husbands or wives. They may even marry a non-Kuwaiti, especially if they spend some time abroad. However, if they do, they are likely to meet with some resistance from their family. According to Kuwaiti law, a female Kuwaiti who marries a non-Kuwaiti loses her Kuwaiti citizenship, including all the financial rewards that come with it. The same law, however, does not apply to a Kuwaiti man married to a foreigner.

At some diwaniyat, guests talk about whatever is on their minds. At others, certain topics—such as sports or politics—guide the conversation. The host of a diwaniyah might even circulate a specific subject for discussion days ahead so his guests have a chance to prepare.

While traditionally only men participated in diwaniyat, in recent years some women have started holding their own. They sometimes invite a male visitor to join them if they believe he has something special to add to the discussion.

Eating In and Eating Out

Much of Kuwaiti social life revolves around mealtimes. At home, meals usually include fruits, vegetables, rice, and fish or shellfish from local markets. Kuwaitis often cook seafood with

Cinnamon Tea

Kuwaitis enjoy drinking a sweet tea flavored with the spice cinnamon. Ask an adult to help you make this simple version of a refreshing drink.

Ingredients

2 cups of water

1 cinnamon stick

Small orange peel (part of the skin of an
  orange, removed using a potato peeler)

2 bags of tea

Sugar to taste

Directions

Place the water, cinnamon stick, and orange peel in a small saucepan. Heat the pan on medium until the water boils. Turn down the heat slightly. Add the tea bags, and let the water simmer for 5 minutes. Remove the pan from the heat, and allow the tea to cool. Remove the peel, cinnamon stick, and tea bags. Pour the tea into a large glass over ice. Add sugar and stir. Enjoy!

a blend of spices, including cardamom, coriander, turmeric, and red pepper. Traditionally, lamb was the most common meat in their diet, but increasingly Kuwaitis are eating grilled beef and chicken. Kuwaitis also enjoy several typical Middle Eastern dishes, such as falafel (fried chickpea patties), hummus (chickpea dip) with vegetables or bread, and ful (fava beans flavored with garlic and lemon).

Because of their history as seafarers, Kuwaitis have long been exposed to foods from other lands. In Kuwait City, hundreds of restaurants offer adventurous diners dishes from just about every known cuisine. Even American fast-food restaurants are very popular in Kuwait.

The first McDonald's restaurant in Kuwait opened in 1994. By 2013, there were sixty-nine McDonald's in the small nation.

Unfortunately, Kuwaitis' love of dining out has had a bad effect on the nation's obesity rate. According to a recent study, about 36 percent of men and 48 percent of women in Kuwait are obese. More than 45 percent of children are either overweight or obese. Kuwait now has an extremely high rate of diabetes, a disease associated with excess weight.

Souqs and Shops

In addition to its many restaurants, Kuwait offers a variety of recreational attractions. In and around Kuwait City there are museums, movie theaters, parks, sports clubs, and theme parks. Visitors to the largest theme park, Entertainment City, can enjoy games, boat rides, miniature golf, and some forty different rides. During the spring, families often venture into the desert for picnics. In the summer, Kuwait's beaches are full of people seeking relief from the soaring heat.

With generous financial support from the national government, Kuwaitis buy clothing, food, and other necessities at souqs, or large outdoor markets. One of the liveliest markets is the huge

Gleaming shopping malls abound in Kuwait.

Souq al-Jum'a (Friday Market). Shoppers there can find anything from Afghan carpets to used books to velvet furniture.

Kuwaitis also enjoy visiting modern shops and boutiques, particularly in air-conditioned shopping malls. The Avenues in Kuwait City is a favorite spot for enthusiastic shoppers. The huge mall has more than eight hundred stores.

One of the biggest events in Kuwait each year is the Hala Shopping Festival. Held in February, the festival draws Kuwaitis into shopping centers with big discounts, special promotions, and valuable door prizes. Older Kuwaitis often complain that their people have become too materialistic, too centered on the luxury goods money can buy. But the Hala Shopping Festival manages to combine the Kuwaitis' shopping mania with a celebration of national pride. At the height of the festival, Kuwaitis observe two important national holidays—National Day, which marks the day they became a nation, and Liberation Day, which commemorates the end of the Iraqi occupation of

Kuwaiti National Holidays

January 1	New Year's Day
February 25	National Day
February 26	Liberation Day

Kuwait also celebrates the following Muslim holidays, which fall on different days of the Western calendar each year:

Mawlid al-Nabi (Birth of the Prophet Muhammad)

Lailat al Miraj (Night of the Ascension of the Prophet Muhammad)

'Id al-Fitr (End of Ramadan)

'Id al-Adha (Feast of Sacrifice)

Islamic New Year

Kuwait in 1991. On these days, as fireworks burst in the sky above Kuwait City, Kuwaitis gather together to celebrate their nation and the rich history and culture they share.

Kuwaitis celebrate National Day by flying flags and large kites.

Timeline

KUWAITI HISTORY		WORLD HISTORY	
Early people build a settlement on Failaka Island in Kuwait Bay.	ca. 2000 BCE	ca. 2500 BCE	The Egyptians build the pyramids and the Sphinx in Giza.
		ca. 563 BCE	The Buddha is born in India.
		313 CE	The Roman emperor Constantine legalizes Christianity.
Muhammad founds Islam, which will become the official religion of Kuwait.	610 CE	610	The Prophet Muhammad begins preaching a new religion called Islam.
		1054	The Eastern (Orthodox) and Western (Roman Catholic) Churches break apart.
		1095	The Crusades begin.
		1215	King John seals the Magna Carta.
		1300s	The Renaissance begins in Italy.
		1347	The plague sweeps through Europe.
		1453	Ottoman Turks capture Constantinople, conquering the Byzantine Empire.
		1492	Columbus arrives in North America.
		1500s	Reformers break away from the Catholic Church, and Protestantism is born.
The Bani Khalid tribe establishes a fishing village at what is now Kuwait City.	Early 1600s		
The Bani Khalid tribe builds a small fort at what is now Kuwait City.	ca. 1672		
Members of the Bani Utub tribe begin migrating to Kuwait.	ca. 1710		
Sabah bin Jaber becomes the first ruler of Kuwait, beginning the reign of the al-Sabah dynasty.	ca. 1756		
		1776	The U.S. Declaration of Independence is signed.
		1789	The French Revolution begins.
		1865	The American Civil War ends.
		1879	The first practical lightbulb is invented.

KUWAITI HISTORY

1896 Mubarak al-Sabah assassinates his brother Muhammad and succeeds him as ruler of Kuwait.

1899 An agreement between Kuwait and Great Britain establishes Kuwait as a British protectorate.

1920 Kuwaiti and British soldiers fight off invaders from Saudi Arabia at the Battle of al-Jahra.

1938 Oil is discovered in Kuwait.

1946 Kuwait's oil industry begins pumping and exporting oil.

1961 Kuwait becomes an independent nation.

1962 Kuwait's constitution goes into effect.

1963 Kuwait holds its first popular election for the National Assembly.

1976 The Kuwaiti government takes control of the nation's oil industry.

1980–1988 Kuwait supports Iraq in the Iran-Iraq War.

1990 Iraq invades Kuwait.

1991 Coalition troops led by the United States liberate Kuwait from the Iraqi occupation.

2006 Kuwaiti women are allowed to vote for the first time.

2011 Young Kuwaitis demonstrate for reforms in the government, inspired by Arab Spring protests in nearby countries.

2012 Opposition leaders and voters boycott national elections because of the government's changes to election laws.

WORLD HISTORY

1914 World War I begins.

1917 The Bolshevik Revolution brings communism to Russia.

1929 A worldwide economic depression begins.

1939 World War II begins.

1945 World War II ends.

1969 Humans land on the moon.

1975 The Vietnam War ends.

1989 The Berlin Wall is torn down as communism crumbles in Eastern Europe.

1991 The Soviet Union breaks into separate states.

2001 Terrorists attack the World Trade Center in New York City and the Pentagon near Washington, D.C.

2004 A tsunami in the Indian Ocean destroys coastlines in Africa, India, and Southeast Asia.

2008 The United States elects its first African American president.

Fast Facts

Official name: State of Kuwait

Capital: Kuwait City

Official language: Arabic

Kuwait City

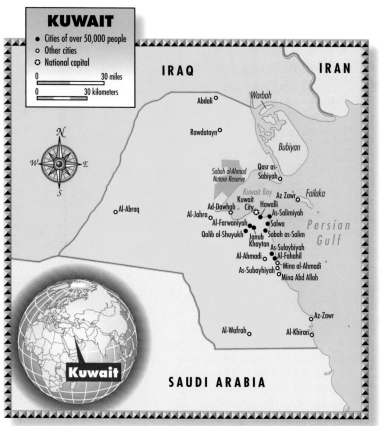

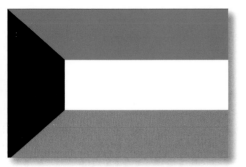

Kuwaiti flag

Official religion:	Islam
Year of founding:	1961
National anthem:	"Al-Nasheed al-Watani" ("National Anthem")
Government:	Constitutional emirate
Head of state:	Emir
Head of government:	Prime minister
Area of country:	6,880 square miles (17,819 sq km)
Latitude and longitude of geographic center:	29° N, 46° E
Bordering countries:	Iraq to the north and west, Saudi Arabia to the south and west
Highest elevation:	Unnamed site, 1,004 feet (306 m) above sea level
Lowest elevation:	Persian Gulf, at sea level
Average daily high temperature:	116°F (47°C) in July; 67°F (19°C) in January
Average daily low temperature:	87°F (31°C) in July; 47°F (8°C) in January
Highest monthly rainfall:	1 inch (2.5 cm) in January
Lowest monthly rainfall:	0 inches (0 cm) in June, July, August, and September

Persian Gulf

Kuwait Towers

Currency

National population (2008 est.):	3,328,136	
Population of major cities (2012 est.):	Kuwait City (metropolitan area)	2,400,000
	Al-Fahahil	74,200
	Al-Ahmadi	41,600
	Al-Jahra	28,400

Landmarks:

▶ *Kuwait House at the National Memorial Museum*, Kuwait City

▶ *Kuwait Towers*, Kuwait City

▶ *Kuwait National Museum*, Kuwait City

▶ *Red Palace*, al-Jahra

▶ *Al-Shamiya Gate*, Kuwait City

Economy: The oil industry is at the center of the Kuwaiti economy. Today, Kuwait produces approximately 2.5 million barrels of oil a day. Recent discoveries of natural gas suggest that exploitation of this valuable resource will become increasingly important in the future. Because of a lack of freshwater and fertile soil, agriculture plays almost no role in Kuwait's economy. Aside from modest amounts of fish and shellfish harvested from the Persian Gulf, Kuwait must import nearly all the food consumed by its people.

Currency: The Kuwaiti dinar. In June 2013, 1 Kuwaiti dinar was worth US$3.53.

System of weights and measures: Metric system

Literacy rate (2007): 93%

Schoolchildren

Common Arabic words and phrases:

Al salaam alaykum	Hello
Ma' al-salama	Good-bye
Tisbah ala-khayr	Good night (to a man)
Tisbinin ala-khayr	Good night (to a woman)
Fursa sa'ida	Pleased to meet you
Kif al-hal?	How are you?
Kif al-'a'ila?	How is your family?
Baraka Allah bik	Thank you
Afwan	You're welcome

Prominent Kuwaitis:

Mishari Rashid Alafasy (1976–)
Imam of the Grand Mosque

Fehaid al-Deehani (1966–)
Olympic shooting champion

Laila al-Othman (1945–)
Novelist and short story writer

Sabah al-Ahmad al-Jaber al-Sabah (1929–)
Emir

Bashar al-Shatti (1984–)
Pop singer

Rola Dashti (1964–)
Politician and activist

Mubarak the Great (1840–1915)
Ruler of Kuwait

Bashar al-Shatti

To Find Out More

Books

▶ DiPiazza, Francesca Davis. *Kuwait in Pictures*. Minneapolis, MN: Twenty-First Century Books, 2007.

▶ O'Shea, Maria, and Michael Spilling. *Kuwait*. 2nd ed. New York: Marshall Cavendish Benchmark, 2010.

▶ Tracy, Kathleen. *We Visit Kuwait*. Hockessin, DE: Mitchell Lane Publishers, 2012.

Music

▶ *Acoustic Arabia*. New York: Putumayo World Music, 2008.

▶ Ensemble Al-Umayri. *The Sawt in Kuwait*. Paris: Institut du Monde Arabe, 2004.

▶ Visit this Scholastic Web site for more information on Kuwait:
www.factsfornow.scholastic.com
Enter the keyword **Kuwait**

Index

Page numbers in *italics*
indicate illustrations.

mining, 78
Modern Art Museum, 112
mosques, 84, 97, *97*, *102*, 105, *105*
al-Mubarak, Massouma, 65–66, *66*
Mubarak the Great, 43, *43*, 44, 45, 65, 133
Muhammad (Islamic prophet), 95, 97, 103, 110
museums, 45, 64, 107–109, 110, *110*, 121
music, 9, 14, 69, *106*, 109–110, 111, *111*, 112
Mutla Ridge, 24

N

al-Naqi, Hamad, 103
national animal, 15, 25, *30*, *34*, *34*, 35, *114*, 115, 119
national anthem, 9, 69
National Assembly, 50, 58, 59, 64, 66–68, *66*, 68, 69, 70, 71, 73, 74, 75, 103, 104, 112
national coat of arms, 84
National Day, 126, 127
national flag, 69, 73, *73*, 116, *127*
national flower, 32, *32*
national holidays, 69, 99, 110, 126–127
National Memorial Museum, 107–108
National Unity Law, 103–104
natural gas, 78, 79
Neutral Zone, 21, *44*
newspapers, 73–74, 103
99, *The* (comic book), 113
99 Village theme park, 113

O

obesity rate, 125
oil industry. *See also* economy.
  al-Ahmadi, 23
  borders and, 45
  cricket and, 116

al-Fahahil, 23, *23*
foreign workers and, 81–82, 90, 114
government and, 14–15, 76, 81
Great Britain and, 46, 116
Gulf War and, 28, *28*, 29, 52, 55
infrastructure and, 46
Kuwait City and, 49, 64
Kuwait Oil Company (KOC), 23, *23*, 46, 47
language and, 91
Neutral Zone, 21
pipelines, *15*, 47
pollution and, 28, *28*
population and, 87
social benefits of, 14–15, 48, 81
United States and, 46
Olympic Games, 116, *116*
al-Othman, Laila, 113, 133
Ottoman Empire, 43
oud (musical instrument), 111

P

Palestine, 48, 82, 88, 112
Parliament, 45, 89
Partitioned Zone. *See* Neutral Zone.
Pearl Diving Festival, 8, 9–10, 11, *11*, 12–13, *12*, 13–14, 16–17, 42
people
  Arabs, 88
  Bani Khalid tribe, 40
  Bani Utub tribe, 41–42
  Bedouins, 25, 34, 40, 41, *41*, 43, 45, 66, 109, *109*
  Bidoon, 89, *89*
  children, 84, 86, 87, *92*, *118*, 120, 122, 125, *127*
  citizenship, 89, 90, 122
  clothing, 9, 80, 98
  Dilmun culture, 38, 39
  diwaniyah ("meeting"), 121–122, *121*
  early settlers, 39

education, 43, 48, 77, 81, 89, 90, 91, 93, *93*, 103, 120, *120*
Failaka Island, 39
families, 8, 57, 73, 80, *118*, 119–120, 122
foods, 26, 61, 81, 91, 97, 98, 99, 99, 121, 122, 124–125, *124*
health care, 43, 48, 77, 81, 87, 125
hospitality of, 120
housing, 15, 81, 119, 121
jobs, 12–13, *12*, 15, 48–49, 77, 81–83, 89, 90, 119
languages, 91–92, *91*, *102*
leisure time, 121–122, *121*, 125
life expectancy, 87
literacy rate, 93
marriage, 57, 72, 122, *122*
median age, 87
modernization and, 16–17
obesity rate, 125
population, 23, 48, 54, 64, 84, 87, 88
refugees, 54, 57
retirement, 81
social rank, 89–91
voting rights, 59, 69–70, *70*, 71, 73
women, *17*, 59, 66, *66*, 70, *70*, 71, *71*, 73, 81, 82, 93, 103, 119, 122
Persian Gulf, 19, 37, 39, 45, 52
plant life
  Arfaj (national flower), 32, *32*
  Bubiyan Island, 22
  climate and, 31
  deserts, 29, 31
  grasses, 31
  Green Island, 32, *32*
  Gulf War and, 28, 29
  halophytes, 31
  al-Jahra, 23, 32
  livestock and, 31

Meet the Author

AGRADUATE OF SWARTHMORE COLLEGE IN Pennsylvania, Liz Sonneborn is a full-time writer living in Brooklyn, New York. She has written more than ninety nonfiction books for both children and adults on a wide variety of subjects. Her works include *The American West, A to Z of American Indian Women, The Ancient Kushites, The Vietnamese Americans, Chronology of American Indian History, Guglielmo Marconi,* and *The Environmental Movement.* Sonneborn has also written numerous books for the Enchantment of the World series, including *Yemen, United Arab Emirates,* and *Iraq.*

Although Sonneborn has written several books for young readers about the Middle East, Kuwait presented some unique challenges. "I've had a few friends who have been employed by Kuwaiti companies," she explains, "so I was familiar with the unique social structure of Kuwait, in which Kuwaiti citizens enjoy a high standard of living, while foreigners, who make up the majority of the population, generally have low incomes and almost no legal protections. In researching this

book, I had to explore what this type of society means for the country, particularly the obstacles it presents in Kuwait's efforts to become a modern and stable nation." Sonneborn relied heavily on Internet news sources to sort out Kuwait's complex and changing social and political situation. "For any researcher," Sonneborn says, "the Internet provides the best and most up-to-date information available on politically volatile regions. For this project, it was particularly useful for getting a sense of how Kuwaitis from a variety of perspectives view their nation and what type of governmental reforms they hope to see in the future."

Photo Credits